Diversity Works

The Emerging Picture of How Students Benefit

Diversity Works

The Emerging Picture of How Students Benefit

Daryl G. Smith

with

Guy L. Gerbick, Mark A. Figueroa, Gayle Harris Watkins,
Thomas Levitan, Leeshawn Cradoc Moore, Pamela A. Merchant,
Haim Dov Beliak, Benjamin Figueroa

Claremont Graduate University

AMERICAN
COMMITMENTS

Association
of American
Colleges and
Universities

AAC&U

Advancing
Liberal
Learning

THIS PUBLICATION WAS PRODUCED WITH SUPPORT FROM THE FORD FOUNDATION
AND IS PUBLISHED AS PART OF THE ASSOCIATION OF AMERICAN COLLEGES AND
UNIVERSITIES' NATIONAL INITIATIVE,
AMERICAN COMMITMENTS: DIVERSITY, DEMOCRACY, AND LIBERAL LEARNING

PUBLISHED BY
ASSOCIATION OF AMERICAN COLLEGES AND UNIVERSITIES
1818 R STREET, NORTHWEST
WASHINGTON, D.C. 20009-1604

ISBN 0-911696-71-7

Contents

Introduction

This report, a literature review and annotated bibliography of research on the impact of campus diversity on American college students, incorporates and extends an earlier study, *The Impact of Diversity on Students: A Preliminary Review of the Research Literature* (1996), conducted by M. Appel, D. Cartwright, D. Smith, and L. Wolf and published by the Association of American Colleges and Universities (AAC&U). That report appeared at a critical time when reliable assessments of diversity programs were needed to guide the continuation of fledgling diversity programs in the face of growing budget cutbacks on campuses and public skepticism of the need for increased support of diversity. It received wide distribution and frequent citation as a valuable summary of the state of the research on the impact of diversity initiatives on college students. The need for research illuminating the results of diversity initiatives has not abated in the past year. The current political climate as evidenced by state referenda like California's Proposition 209 and legal decisions like Hopwood v. University of Texas confirm the need to document exactly what the educational value of diversity is to higher education.

While the prior study offered a preliminary review of the research, the current review and bibliography, compiled over several months by an expanded staff of researchers, provides a more complete picture of the burgeoning literature in this field. This study also fills some of the gaps identified in the original publication regarding specific student populations and avenues of research. This is not, however, an exhaustive compilation of the literature on diversity's impact on students. New information is published daily and other studies also hold valuable references and insights on this topic (e.g. Hurtado, Milem, Allen, and Clayton-Pedersen 1996).

The core purpose of this expanded and revised edition is to gather recent reports of the student outcomes of intentional programs by colleges and universities to engage issues of diversity on their campuses. While much recently published research builds on earlier important studies, our focus has been on literature published since 1992.

During our search in this increasingly prolific field, we have used the mantra "the *impact* of *diversity* on *students*" as our theme. We therefore focus primarily on reports that meet our research criteria of "the impact of diversity on students"—outcome measures, college students, and recent intentional diversity initiatives. The research reviewed here ranges from quantitative studies using large national data bases of thousands of students to research about a particular program using case studies of a handful of students. If a report summarizes students' observations of the effects of diversity initiatives on them, cites the effect of faculty diversity issues on students, or reports student thinking about the value of a program, we include it in our bibliography. However, research on diversifying the faculty, personal opinion pieces not grounded in research, and descriptions of programs that do not measure or report their effects on students were generally excluded. While most of the research we cite fits all the criteria, we also include some studies that are foundational analyses of diversity, report research-based strategies to increase diversity, focus on specific populations of students that have traditionally been underrepresented in the literature, or report the effects of the lack of diversity on students.

While we have attempted to gather all literature reporting outcome measures of diversity programs on college campuses, many programs considered highly successful do not formally evaluate their impact on students. Or, if they do, they do not make these findings available outside their university community. To expand and deepen knowledge about the field, we encourage campuses to evaluate and widely report the outcomes of their diversity work in this area. Both positive and negative outcomes will help other colleges and universities design appropriate strategies for their students. One forum for exchanging such information is an exciting new website, DiversityWeb, developed by the Association of American Colleges and Universities in collaboration with the University of Maryland. DiversityWeb is available at http://www.inform.umd.edu/diversityweb.

As our title suggests, the landscape of this research is becoming more clear each day, but many pieces of the picture still remain hazy. Contributions from both researchers and practitioners are imperative if we are to increase the focus, composition, and balance of the picture.

Authors' Acknowledgments

A ll of the authors would like to express their deep appreciation to a very supportive advisory group who added to the eyes and ears of the research team for work that needed to be included. The advisory panel included Mildred García, Sylvia Hurtado, Shirley Hune, Lisa Wolf Wendel.

A report like this one reflects the hard work and commitment of many whose work often goes unnoticed. We appreciate especially the efforts of the staff of the Association of American Colleges and Universities, including Carol Schneider, Caryn McTighe Musil, Lee Knefelkamp, Debra Humphreys, Kenneth Krattenmaker and Ben Plimpton. The preparation of the manuscript became a truly collaborative effort in keeping with the commitments driving this publication. This report could not have been possible without the commitment of Edgar Beckham at The Ford Foundation, Carol Schneider at AAC&U, and the Claremont Graduate University.

I am particularly grateful to work with a wonderful team of students who made this report possible.

Daryl G. Smith
Claremont Graduate University
August, 1997

Executive Summary

In reviewing research on the impact of diversity on students in higher education, we have combed research reports from numerous sources to compose a picture of our current understanding of the value to students of diversity on campus. While many studies reviewed for this report evaluate the practices employed by individual institutions and their programs, others use national databases and multi-institutional studies to provide an empirical foundation for the development of individual initiatives.

Over time, the research traces a movement from focused concern for the access, retention, and success of underrepresented students in higher education to broader concerns about the effects of increasing demographic, cultural, and social changes on the educational context as a whole—campus services, intergroup relations, pedagogy, the curriculum, and institutional purpose. While concern for the continuing underrepresentation of certain groups of students remains high on the research and institutional agenda, the analysis of campus diversity now also includes new developments in climate, curriculum, scholarship, institutional practice, and mission. As fundamental changes resulting from societal diversity are felt throughout an institution and its constituencies, multi-faceted and ongoing evaluations of the impact of these changes become essential.

Campus leaders are also exploring what institutional changes are needed to successfully educate a diverse student body to live, work, and excel in a complex and pluralistic society. These changes mean more than just the successful adjustment of new categories of students to a given institution. They include as well how institutions must be altered if they are to better educate and prepare all students for a changing world.

While conclusions about successful strategies for implementing broad-based changes are preliminary, the published research literature nonetheless warrants a number of statements about "what works" in campus diversity efforts.

1. Overall, the literature suggests that diversity initiatives positively affect both minority and majority students on campus. Significantly, diversity initiatives have an impact not only on student attitudes and feelings toward intergroup relations on campus, but also on institutional satisfaction, involvement, and academic growth.

2. Programs which focus on the transition to college are important for the recruitment, retention, and academic success of underrepresented students. The apparent success of honors approaches for at-risk students suggests that the differences between cultural and academic transitions need to be clearly addressed in the design of transitional and special support programs.

3. Mentoring programs, involving both student peers and faculty, consistently result in improved adjustment, retention, and academic success rates for their participants. Faculty involvement with students produces similar results.

4. The evidence grows showing that involvement in specialized student groups, such as ethnic residential theme houses, support centers, and academic departments benefits students of color and others. Indeed, these activities appear to contribute to increased satisfaction and retention, despite prodigious commentary of their negative effect on the development of community on campus.

5. Though specialized student support programs and campus community have been pitted against each other, research results suggest that institutional commitment to both contributes to the educational success of all students. These findings underscore the capacity of individuals, groups, and institutions to thrive through an acknowledgment of multiple affiliations and identities on campus.

6. Contrary to widespread reports of self-segregation among students of color on campuses, the research finds this pattern more typical of white students. Students of color interact more with dominant students than the reverse.

7. Opportunities for interaction between and among student groups are desired by virtually all students and produce clear increases in understanding and decreases in prejudicial attitudes. Such opportunities also positively affect academic success. The conditions under which interactions among individuals are likely to be beneficial include institutional support, equal status, and common goals.

8. Increasing numbers of campuses are recognizing the significance of creating opportunities for intergroup dialogue as part of diversity efforts. However, the conditions for effective dialogue cannot be assumed and the necessity of sustaining difficult dialogues has become increasingly urgent. There appear to be significant numbers of instances where institutions and groups are "talking past" one another. While the literature reviewed here focuses on campus initiatives with students, it is likely that evaluating the conditions for dialogue among other constituencies, including faculty and administrators, is equally important.

9. The evidence continues to grow that serious engagement of issues of diversity in the curriculum and in the classroom has a positive impact on attitudes toward racial issues, on opportunities to interact in deeper ways with those who are different, on cognitive development, and on overall satisfaction and involvement with the institution. These benefits are particularly powerful for white students who have had less opportunity for such engagement.

10. Recent research on the significance of the institutional commitment to diversity suggests that the perception of a broad campus commitment to diversity is related to increased recruitment and retention of students from under-represented groups.

11. This perception of a broad campus commitment to diversity is also related to positive educational outcomes for *all* students, individual satisfaction, and a commitment to improving racial understanding.

12. Evidence in the literature suggests that comprehensive institutional change in teaching methods, curriculum, campus climate, and institutional definition provides educational benefits for both minority and majority students. Comprehensive diversity initiatives, beyond their capacity to improve access and retention for underrepresented groups, are related to satisfaction, academic success, and cognitive development for *all* students.

13. Special mission institutions—historically black colleges and universities (HBCU's), American Indian controlled colleges, women's colleges, and Latino/a serving institutions are important in higher education for the student groups they serve. High expectations, belief in students' ability to succeed, community involvement, and the presence of role models seem to play crucial parts in their well-documented success.

14. While reports of successful diversity initiatives are encouraging, more cross-institutional studies are needed. Moreover, the deeper studies which are emerging from individual campuses will continue to expand what we know about effective strategies, about the differential impact of certain strategies for different student groups, and about the apparent relationship between addressing the needs of underrepresented students through particular programs and initiatives, while at the same time addressing institutional issues through broad based strategies.

15. We also need more clear analysis of what students need to know and do to function in a diverse workplace and global society, and what part they can play in developing healthy, respectful communities.

Part I

New Frameworks for Studying Diversity in Higher Education

1

The Context for Campus Diversity Research

Higher education has been actively addressing campus diversity issues since the 1960s. The earliest efforts were aimed almost entirely at providing access for groups of students who had previously been excluded because of their gender, race, and/or ethnicity. Three decades later, the issue of access is still with us. In addition to concern about equitable access, however, there is also concern about the educational persistence and success of underrepresented populations. These concerns are compounded by increasing incidents of hostility directed toward students of color, Jewish students, gays and lesbians, and others. As a result, campuses all over the country are asking questions about how the academy can best fulfill its role in educating both previously included and excluded populations for a rapidly changing society. Consequently, there have been new efforts throughout higher education to develop a broad variety of programs and initiatives addressing access and equity, student success, campus climate, intergroup relations, curriculum, scholarship, and institutional mission.

> CAMPUSES OF ALL KINDS SERVE AS A MICROCOSM FOR THE ISSUES, EFFORTS, AND TENSIONS BEING PLAYED OUT ELSEWHERE IN SOCIETY.

It is now publicly acknowledged that campus diversity efforts are also directly related to larger societal issues. As the demographics of the United States become more diverse and as economic and political issues become global rather than local, it is increasingly apparent that issues of diversity are central not only to our campuses but to cities, communities, and to a healthy civic democracy. Colleges and universities, pressed by both internal and external constituencies, are inevitably being called upon to clarify the larger relationship between higher education and society. At the same time, campuses of all kinds serve as a microcosm for the issues, efforts, and tensions being played out elsewhere in society. Few, if any, in our institutions and in our society have participated in fully pluralistic and equitable communities. Thus, higher education is learning, innovating, and changing while facing a largely unprecedented challenge.

Given the magnitude of the issues, it is not surprising that campus efforts at diversity are confronted with and affected by national and local political, legal, and economic challenges. For some, campus diversity efforts have clearly not been supported at levels sufficient to produce tangible results. For others, these efforts are by definition divisive, illegal, and ineffective. Our study responds to these basic questions about campus diversity practices. Our review of the research seeks to answer questions about the impact of these efforts upon students. At the same time, we hope our report will deepen people's understanding about how to create educational and intellectual environments appropriate for a pluralistic society.

In the contested terrain that is diversity today, it is imperative that we document and describe what is happening on our campuses educationally and that we garner evidence which illuminates the results of campus diversity efforts. It is especially vital that we begin to understand the conditions under which campus diversity initiatives will be successful and the conditions that do not foster success. Many people have personal notions about what will "bring people together" or about viable educational practices. These questions need to be studied empirically. It is also clear that empirically validated information is vital to sustaining the commitment and efforts of institutions to educate students from and for a diverse society.

No single study or methodology will answer the complex set of questions that confront institutions laboring to educate students from and for a diverse society. Moreover, research on diversity cannot be disconnected from history and context. Nor can it be separated from the individuals and institutions implementing changes. Some progress has been made in moving away from narrowly conceived deficit models that presume that if students fail, it must be because of student limitations. Using a much wider array of research methodologies, often combining qualitative and quantitative methods, studies are now more frequently considering other possible factors that might influence student success: the curriculum, pedagogy, or campus climate. Pulling together literatures with disparate methodologies conducted in myriad locations creates an opportunity to see whether, in the aggregate, conclusions can be drawn that assist in the discussions and decisions taking place. This task mirrors the complexity of diversity in American higher education and makes generalizations more difficult. It is one hope of this report that more specific research will be conducted in the areas discussed in later chapters.

IT IS ESPECIALLY VITAL THAT WE BEGIN TO UNDERSTAND THE CONDITIONS UNDER WHICH CAMPUS DIVERSITY INITIATIVES WILL BE SUCCESSFUL AND THE CONDITIONS THAT DO NOT FOSTER SUCCESS.

While the research base on campus diversity issues has enlarged in the last year, there is much more to be done. The development of this emerging field will depend on both complex national studies and the efforts of campus-based researchers and practitioners sharing the results of local studies. While it is beyond the scope of this report to suggest how such studies might be done, other theoretical and applied literature is available to guide those efforts (e.g. Astin 1991, 1993; Banta 1993; California Postsecondary Education Commission 1992; Nettles 1990b; Smith, Wolf, and Levitan 1994; Tierney

1990, 1993). The literature reviewed also provides many models for additional research.

The following chapters attempt to pull together a broad range of studies representing a wide variety of methodologies. Taken together, this body of research underscores the conclusion that attending to issues of diversity is positively related to student success, and, thus, is directly related to educational excellence. Moreover, the studies reveal that higher education is on the right path by addressing diversity in multiple ways at all levels of institutions.

2

A Framework for Analysis:
Searching and Organizing the Literature

Diversity is a broad term that holds both multiple and politically contentious meanings in higher education (Adelman 1997). Frequently used terms such as multicultural, multiethnic, underrepresented, minority, disadvantaged, marginalized or stigmatized are also contentious, even as they provide conceptual nets for filtering the broad literature on diversity.

In another report previously published by AAC&U, the authors describe diversity as "the variety created in any society (and within any individual) by the presence of different points of view and ways of making meaning which generally flow from the influence of different cultural and religious heritages, from the differences in how we socialize women and men, and from the differences that emerge from class, age and developed ability." (AAC&U 1995). Seen this way, diversity on campus encompasses complex differences within the campus community and also in the individuals who compose that community. It includes such important and intersecting dimensions of human identity as race, ethnicity, national origin, religion, gender, sexual orientation, class, age and ability. These dimensions do not determine or predict any one person's values, orientation, choices, or responses. But they are by definition closely related to patterns of societal experience, socialization and affiliation. They influence ways of understanding and interpreting the world.

Acknowledging these complex and intersecting influences on any one person's perceptual frameworks underscores the point that there are multiple ways to view the world, both emotionally and intellectually. Acknowledging the significance of diverse identities and societal experiences also helps illuminate the range of issues with which students struggle, both interpersonally and academically, as they become participants in campus educational communities that are frequently far more heterogeneous than any they have previously experienced.

Diversity in higher education has also come to mean, however, not just the differences among and between peoples, but also the value and significance that a community places on particular differences. Social identities and affinities emerge as significant, in part, because of the asymmetrical cultural and historical contexts in which they have been placed. Until the 1960s, the great majority of American colleges and universities were overwhelmingly white. Minority students were rarely seen; their cultural traditions were almost entirely excluded from both the formal curriculum and the informal campus culture. Many institutions sustained quotas on specific religious groups. Other campuses either excluded or subordinated women while virtually every institution denigrated homosexuality. For students from less privileged economic and/or cultural backgrounds, class was—and remains still—a difficult and often painful issue.

These histories, affecting institutions and individuals alike, have created the contexts in which contemporary campus diversity efforts function. They frame and influence the goals leaders of these efforts are attempting to achieve. They also help account for differential responses to the same program, experience or event by different members of the community.

Campus diversity is more, however, than a list of communal traditions and experiences with which individuals may identify and to which others may react. The term "campus diversity" has also come to refer to the variety of strategies institutions and leaders have developed to address the consequences of earlier homogeneity both at a particular institution and in higher education generally. Adelman (1997) notes this variety when he observes that campus diversity means different things depending on the observer. For some it is a code word for the presence of designated and previously excluded groups; for others it is a climate that welcomes heterogeneity; for still others it is a range of programs designed to influence what and how students learn. For many it is all of these things simultaneously.

Given the variety of diversities on campus (and in society) and the disparate actions that higher education is taking to address diversity, it is clear that we cannot use uni-dimensional conceptions to define research into the effects of campus diversity on students. For example, does diversity refer only to African Americans and Latino/as, or does it include white women? How inclusive should a study of campus climate be? What role do Asian Americans play in diversity conversations? Are gay and lesbian concerns integral to campus diversity issues? When we talk about campus diversity efforts, are we describing programs for particular groups? For any group that feels distinctive or marginal? For all students? For everyone in the campus community—faculty, staff and administrators as well as students? How do communities outside the campus relate to campus diversity issues and groups?

Because of the inherent complexity of the topic, we believe it is necessary to examine *multiple* dimensions of diversity in higher education. The benefit of a multidimensional approach is that it allows us to examine a range of strategies currently used in higher education both to address the needs of diverse students and also to help institutions adjust to the reality of increased heterogeneity on campus and in the larger society. Rather than hold institutions to a restrictive definition of campus diversity efforts, the approach we take here recognizes the multiplicity of efforts now underway to engage societal differences in educational contexts. Using a multidimensional approach proves to be a useful way of organizing and assessing the rapidly expanding research literature on students' experiences with diversity. It also allows us to acknowledge the continuing evolution of the very phrase, "campus diversity."

In what follows, we have used four distinct though interrelated dimensions of campus diversity to search and interpret campus diversity research (see figure). The framework has been developed by Smith (1995) and elaborated in earlier studies. We summarize the several dimensions of the framework and the rationale for their use below.

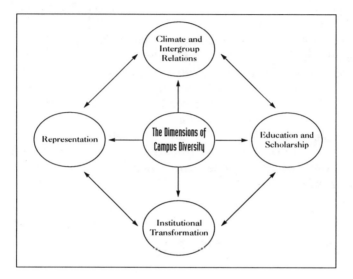

Representation

The first dimension, *representation*, focuses on the inclusion and success of previously underrepresented groups. This is the most commonly understood element of diversity initiatives, and it has emerged from a social and historical context of exclusion and resulting underrepresentation. Thirty years ago, higher education greatly accelerated efforts to lower barriers for groups that had been formerly excluded. The focus of these efforts over time has been on underrepresented students of color, particularly African American, Latino/a and American Indian students, and white women. This focus has defined the efforts of the modern affirmative action movement in which a wide variety of programs have been put in place to redress past discrimination. These efforts to increase access have been conceptualized in terms of social justice and equity. Today when women comprise a majority of the undergraduate student population, access by gender is no longer a dominant issue, except in certain fields or in rare instances such as the Citadel or Virginia Military Institute, both of which had denied women access until ordered by the courts to admit them. Gender becomes a factor more frequently in the current situation as it is linked with continuing racial barriers to access.

In this first dimension, then, attention is paid most typically in the nineties to the access and success of African American men and women, Latino/as, and American Indians. For many years, less notice was given to Asian American students. Because they were labeled as the "model minority," issues of representation and success were often ignored. Today, as we come to understand more about the diversity *among* Asian Americans and about the variety of challenges they face, more attention is being paid and will have to be paid to issues of representation and success for that community as well (Hune and Chan 1997).

While colleges and universities began by comparing institutional numbers with the demographic distribution of populations in the country and by region, it became clear that focusing simply on numbers at entrance was not sufficient and that student success was the important goal. Here, too, numbers are often used to indicate institutional outcomes. Thus, elements within this dimension include access data, affirmative action, targeted financial aid programs, high school to college bridge programs, retention, graduation, mentoring, and other efforts intended to address both inclusion and academic success for those who are or have previously been underrepresented. This dimension remains basic to other facets of campus diversity.

Campus Climate and Intergroup Relations

The second dimension, *campus climate and intergroup relations*, addresses the impact of the collegiate environment on institutional and student success. It includes activities which seek to prevent students from experiencing campuses as alienating, hostile, and "chilly." At the extreme of the spectrum, campuses have had to address hate crimes, racism, gay-bashing, anti-semitism, as well as charges that much is lacking for students with physical and learning abilities. More typically, however, climate issues are less dramatic. It is more a matter of assessing the accrual of smaller, more subtle factors that nonetheless can create a negative learning environment for many groups of students. This second dimension, then, expands beyond those groups historically denied access to embrace a far broader group of students. As campuses have broadened their diversity concerns, another shift has occurred. Studying the climate of a campus begins to expand from a focus on specific groups of students and what "they" might need, to include studying institutional characteristics that affect the psychosocial environment and therefore may influence all students' experiences, levels of involvement, and academic achievement.

Increasing diversity on many campuses and the very visibility of diversity have also prompted attention to the ways in which the climate supports and develops intergroup relations between and among groups. While framed often in ways which seem to blame students of color for finding support from one another, the current efforts to develop opportunities for genuine intergroup dialogue have important implications for campuses as well as for society. Campuses have a unique opportunity to create intergroup dialogues in a variety of forums. Thus, efforts concerning campus climate and intergroup relations are very significant dimensions of diversity today and continue to involve complex issues, including legacies of intolerance and racism.

Education and Scholarship

The third dimension of the framework, *education and scholarship*, involves the inclusion of diverse traditions in the curriculum, the impact of issues of diversity on teaching methods, and the influence of societal diversity on scholarly inquiry. The core of higher education is made up of: 1) the curriculum—what we teach; 2) pedagogy—how we teach it; and, 3) scholarly inquiry—what we value. Perceiving that the curriculum was connected to student success, and recognizing that much had been omitted from traditional academic fields, many campus diversity efforts have focused on the curriculum. The development of ethnic studies and women's studies provided the intellectual basis for these efforts. Similarly, as researchers drew attention to often "chilly" campus climates, many campuses turned to the classroom as a place to teach about tolerance, inclusion, and structural inequities in society.

> AS RESEARCHERS DREW ATTENTION TO OFTEN "CHILLY" CAMPUS CLIMATES, MANY CAMPUSES TURNED TO THE CLASSROOM AS A PLACE TO TEACH ABOUT TOLERANCE, INCLUSION, AND STRUCTURAL INEQUITIES IN SOCIETY.

With the changing demographics of the country, the increased globalization of the economy, and the continuing evidence of intolerance and inequities, many campuses have begun to conclude that educating *all* students for a diverse society and world is part of an emerging institutional mission—one from which all students might benefit and, one for which having students from diverse backgrounds is a genuine asset. The most current set of initiatives focusing on the curriculum, then, respond to significant developments in scholarship, the demands for new knowledge in a pluralistic society, and to calls for new capacities for intercultural understanding in all students.

We might see these discussions about the inclusion of diversity from the educational point of view as parallel to discussions about computing in the academy (Smith 1995). Fifteen years ago, knowledge of computers and the use of e-mail and the Internet were peripheral for most students (and faculty). Now, as educators, we have come to assume that students require knowledge of these *tools* to function effectively both in college and after graduation. As computer literacy has been embraced, so must the challenge of educating everyone for living in a multicultural world. The activities related to diversity in the *educational* dimension expand, then, to include all students. The imperative here is the education of students to live in and contribute to a pluralistic society. As such, this dimension sees diversity as central to teaching and learning, not just because some students may require new approaches, but because what and how we need to be teaching has changed.

Institutional Transformation

The fourth and final dimension, *institutional transformation*, refers to deep, reorganizing questions which build upon the many changes prompted in the earlier dimensions. The many "diversity activities" on campus necessarily raise questions about traditional practices and approaches. Indeed, it is clear that a focus on diversity often raises issues which have needed attention for some time. Student success in the form of graduation rates, the significance of mentors, the campus climate for many students, issues of community, intergroup and intragroup relations, links between in-class and out-of-class learning have been concerns for years in higher education. Recent diversity efforts, taken seriously from an institutional point of view, can prompt fundamental improvements in these areas. This fourth dimension includes institutional commitments to diversity as evidenced in leadership and mission statements. Issues of what constitutes scholarship and linkages between communities outside as well as inside the academy are also important transformational elements. Guiding the analysis of this dimension is the fundamental question, "What would our institution look like if we were truly educating a diverse student body to live and work in a pluralistic society?" (Smith 1995). Repercussions from this question continue to transform and focus institutional issues far beyond simply changing institutional patterns of representation, the first dimension in our series.

GUIDING THE ANALYSIS OF THIS DIMENSION IS THE FUNDAMENTAL QUESTION, "WHAT WOULD OUR INSTITUTION LOOK LIKE IF WE WERE TRULY EDUCATING A DIVERSE STUDENT BODY TO LIVE AND WORK IN A PLURALISTIC SOCIETY?"

These four dimensions, then, provide a way of seeing both who "diversity" includes, whom it affects, and how its impact extends beyond individual groups being added or an individual institution becoming more diverse. This framing of the dimensions of diversity also illuminates how the meaning of diversity changes over time as formerly underrepresented groups are brought into higher education and as expectations about the roles they will play develop.

Some campuses are engaging one or two of these dimensions; others are addressing them all, often simultaneously. Thus, conversations about diversity are complex because each dimension highlights different agendas and has different emphases and constituencies. In general, however, such efforts underscore important examples of effective practice for student and institutional success. Each of the dimensions, then, reinforces the others and creates a potential for systemic institutional change.

The dimensions also reveal how interconnected relationships are among diversity initiatives. The first, where the discussions of diversity typically start, is *access*—the ability of historically underrepresented groups of students to participate in the opportunity of higher education. We traditionally think of the principal beneficiary of access as the group that has been previously denied access. Yet, empirical research demonstrates that others benefit as well. There is value for *all* students from participating in diverse institutions. The second is *climate*—both perceived and tangible, the sensed and measurable feeling about a campus and whether an individual or group is included or excluded. Similar to access, the value of an open and accepting climate creates an improved learning environment for *all* students. There is also the *educational* aspect of diversity—both what we choose to teach and how we choose to teach it. Because we see the world in a different way as a result of a growing understanding of diversity, both what we teach and how we teach it change to the benefit of all students—especially those who have had little exposure to these issues. As the demographics of the society shift and as the boundaries between regional and global communities blur, institutional viability and explicit success as well as societal health will depend, in part, on the success of higher education in this effort. Even a cursory overview of each of the changes suggested by what is being learned as principles of good practice for diverse institutions, reveals that these changes generally improve the quality and capacity of the educational experience for all students—and ultimately for the institution as well.

Some people worry that all the institutional lip service to diversity is little more than a rhetorical smoke screen designed to obscure the continuing barriers faced by underrepresented and historically excluded groups in higher education, even as campuses proudly proclaim their attention to diverse groups (Myers 1997). We are cognizant of this issue. While we use a broadly inclusive definition that addresses multiple dimensions of societal diversity, the dimensions allow our study to focus appropriately on multiple efforts designed to support the presence, experience, retention, and success of underrepresented groups on campus. We also focus on efforts to change institutions as a whole so that diversity becomes an educational resource for all students (and others in the community) and so that the institution, itself, is more adequately positioned to serve a changing society.

THERE IS VALUE FOR ALL STUDENTS FROM PARTICIPATING IN DIVERSE INSTITUTIONS.

The issue of terminology also arises concerning the naming of racial groups. For consistency and respect for current patterns of racial self-identification, we have used African American, Latino/a, American Indian, Asian American, and white throughout this study. In the bibliography, where authors used specific terms for describing groups, we followed their language. We also acknowledge the absence of Pacific Islanders and Alaskan Natives, who were not explicitly addressed in the compiled literature.

Throughout our review we found a variety of purposes for diversity efforts, and therefore different types of diversity efforts. Some reports describe educational and support efforts implemented as programs targeted for specific populations that have been historically underrepresented in higher education. Others examine efforts to influence attitudes and change among the majority or overall student population. Some reports focus on institutional factors to increase support, including specific student services, pedagogical methods, or the overall university climate. Still other reports demonstrate the positive impact that a diverse institution has on the learning of all students. What is strikingly common to all of these reports is the cumulative evidence that diversity has a positive impact on students in higher education.

Having identified the relevant literature, we then needed to decide how to organize it into a format useful for researchers interested in this field and to practitioners searching for a program design to enhance the admission, success, and climate for a diverse student body. We have therefore sought to devise an organization of the research that meets both needs. Readers may discern epistemological trends in the literature over time consistent with the dimensions described above. The trend has been to enlarge the concept of diversity from numbers and access to retention studies, to special services for particular groups to improve campus climate, to reports of efforts to reconfigure the curriculum and its pedagogy, and finally to rethink institutional assumptions and structures. Other groupings are also apparent, including student group characteristics, program type, outcome measures, or principles being tested by the research. We have grouped the literature based on common research patterns and questions within one overall schema which addresses directly the multiple and changing meanings of diversity in higher education.

> WHAT IS STRIKINGLY COMMON TO ALL OF THESE REPORTS IS THE CUMULATIVE EVIDENCE THAT DIVERSITY HAS A POSITIVE IMPACT ON STUDENTS IN HIGHER EDUCATION.

Part II

The Research Findings

Part II of this report reviews the research literature organized around the dimensions of diversity described above. Sub-sections within those four categories present commonalities of research that conform to questions frequently asked of institutional leaders and educators:

What difference do all these diversity initiatives make for students in general, and for those in particular student groups?

What programs or factors are most effective in the success of underrepresented students?

What role does the campus climate play in student success?

Are student groups really segregating themselves from one another?

What is known about intergroup relations?

What difference does diversifying the curriculum make?

The theme of involvement on campus and in one's education surfaces repeatedly in this literature review. A clear pattern emerges from this literature which is consistent with much previous work (Astin 1984, 1993; Pascarella & Terenzini 1991; Tinto 1993). Involvement itself appears to positively influence student success. By "involvement," we mean the collection of behaviors and activities in which students are engaged that increases their interaction with other students and with the institution. Researchers have used a wide variety of indicators to assess student involvement. Involvement may refer to participation in student organizations and clubs as leaders or members; attendance at academic, cultural, or social activities; employment on campus in a student job; participation in a varsity or intramural sport; or use of the library, athletic facilities, and labs. Many studies also focus on out-of-class interaction with faculty to assess academic involvement.

3

Representation: Inclusion and Success of Underrepresented Populations

The representational dimension of diversity research includes studies which explore a central purpose of diversity initiatives: access, inclusion, retention, and success of students from underrepresented groups. This section of our report examines literature which focuses on particular student groups and their representation within the academy, and strategies designed to improve their participation and success. These strategies include approaches to increasing initial student enrollment in higher education and activities that work to improve rates of student persistence to the degree by enhancing the academic or the social/emotional experience for students who are underrepresented in higher education. These studies look at the impact of factors and activities ranging from financial aid to academic approaches to mentoring. This study does not look at the current demographics of enrollment in higher education—that data is well summarized elsewhere (Carter and Wilson 1997).

Overall, the literature on the participation of underrepresented students in higher education points to both continuing progress and enduring problems. As access to American colleges and universities increased with the advent of affirmative action, the expansion of public higher education, and the changing demographics of the United States, both the raw numbers and the proportion of racial minority students in higher education institutions have similarly increased (Andrew and Russo 1989; Carter and Wilson 1997). Yet, the participation and success rate for specific populations and in certain degree programs relative to their white peers remains disturbingly low. Clearly, understanding access for specific populations and the conditions which contribute to certain groups of students dropping out must be topics of continuing concern. Some of the programs reviewed in this document identify approaches to remedy these problems.

The apparent exception to this pattern is among Asian American students who have achieved rapid progress in higher education, leading to an all-embracing stereotype of Asian students as the "model minority" (Nagasawa and Espinoza 1992). However, when examined closely by separate nationalities, immigration history, and campus experience, specific groups of Asian and Asian American students continue to experience barriers common to other racial minorities (Hune 1997; Hune and Chan 1997; Osajima 1995).

Improving Access and Retention

Several approaches have been employed to investigate campus efforts to increase access to and persistence in higher education. Some studies, such as that by Mow and Nettles (1993), seek to capture the breadth of the literature and examine trends in the experiences of students of color. Other authors, such as Nelson (1994) and Nora (1987, 1990) look at the extent to which specific factors, such as institutional assistance and financial aid, play a part in the retention of underrepresented students. St. John (1991) examines the role of student financial assistance in access and retention issues, particularly for first-generation college students. This study supports the notion that student financial assistance has a positive impact on access to and persistence in higher education. An increased proportion of loan aid relative to grant aid was found to negatively influence students' decisions to attend college, to persist, and to choose among a wide range of institutions. Similar results are reported by Andrew and Russo (1989).

> WHEN EXAMINED CLOSELY BY SEPARATE NATIONALITIES, IMMIGRATION HISTORY, AND CAMPUS EXPERIENCE, SPECIFIC GROUPS OF ASIAN AND ASIAN AMERICAN STUDENTS CONTINUE TO EXPERIENCE BARRIERS COMMON TO OTHER RACIAL MINORITIES.

Three recent studies examine the genesis and current state of tribally controlled community colleges and their efforts to increase American Indian participation in higher education (Belgarde 1992; Boyer 1997; Carnegie Foundation for the Advancement of Teaching 1989). These colleges, and their counterparts in historically black and Latino/a serving institutions, play a significant role in access to higher education for the groups they serve. The influence of these colleges and universities is further explored in the discussion of institutional transformation in Chapter 6. Several reports also describe pathways designed to increase underrepresented student group participation in predominantly white colleges and universities (Lang and Ford 1992). Gilbert (1996) describes a successful cooperative program between Northern Arizona University and students in seven high schools on or near Navajo and Hopi reservations.

Perhaps the most dramatic contribution to improvement in rates of success has come from Treisman's reorientation of work with students in mathematics programs. This approach, now being adapted in other disciplines, replaces a deficit model (i.e. a model that attempts only to eliminate inadequacies in students) with an "honors" program model characterized by high expectations (i.e. a model that assumes that students are smart and can all achieve). It has proven very successful for formerly "at-risk" students (Conciatore 1990; Fullilove and Treisman 1990). One of the reports on this approach (Asera and Treisman 1995) uses retrospective interviews with high-achieving African American, Latino/a, and American Indian students to examine how students who are considering, or are enrolled in, advanced study in mathematics decided to pursue this path. Similarities among participants who persist included support from family members to achieve academically, early achievement and interest in mathematics, and high school teachers who demonstrated a personal interest in students' success.

Bonsangue and Drew's (1995) study focuses on the effects of a specially designed workshop for Latino/a and African American students in chemistry, physics, and mechanical engineering. Students attended at least one calculus workshop while enrolled in a traditional lecture course in these areas. This group was compared to students who were not enrolled in the workshop. Fifty percent of the non-workshop participants left the institution in three years, while only fifteen percent of the workshop participants left. Ninety-one percent of the workshop students continued in the field of science, math, or engineering, as compared to only forty-two percent of the non-workshop participants who continued in these fields. Also, the course completion rate for African American and Latino/a students in the workshop was ninety-one percent as compared to eighty-two percent of the white students and eighty-nine percent for Asian American students of the non-workshop group.

One program designed to minimize drop-out rates among Latino/a students in community colleges is the Puente Project. McGrath and Galaviz (1996) report on this project which works with students on campus in the context of their families and their culture. The project tries to create an on-campus climate that nurtures students' development along with their academic success. Capoor and Overstreet (1993) track persistence and grade point averages for students participating in programs designed to assist high-risk and under-prepared students with the transition to college. Their results show that tutoring and basic skills instruction are most strongly associated with both measures of success, while a college survival course, taken with no other interventions is least strongly associated with success.

SEVERAL EXPERIMENTAL STUDIES FORCEFULLY DEMONSTRATE THAT VULNERABILITY TO STEREOTYPES IS A MAJOR FACTOR IN ACADEMIC ACHIEVEMENT.

Several experimental studies (Steele 1995, 1997; Steele and Aronson 1995) forcefully demonstrate that vulnerability to stereotypes is a major factor in academic achievement. These studies consistently show that the distraction and apprehension that come from stereotype vulnerability can have a measurable effect on African American students' standardized test performance. Similar results appear for white women in mathematics. The fear of being stereotyped is so "self threatening" that it has negative consequences for performance. From these strong research results, Steele has developed a freshman transition program at the University of Michigan in which students from a variety of backgrounds are introduced to the campus through honors course work, workshops, discussions, and public service. After four years, the racial gap in grades has been eliminated and comparisons to randomized control groups are very positive. The retention rate of African American students in this program is approximately ninety-two percent compared to the seventy percent graduation rate for African Americans in the university at large (Hummel 1997; Hummel and Steele 1996).

Much research on the impact of advising students with learning disabilities has also been published. One study by Vogel and Adelman (1992) compares the educational attainment of students with learning disabilities to a sample of peers matched on gender and ACT composite scores. They found that the college exit grade point average and graduation rate of the learning disabled group was not significantly different from the control group, even though the control group had higher entering reading and written language skills. This finding is attributed to a strong advising system for students with learning disabilities. The study also reveals that the learning disabled group took a lighter academic load and one year longer, six rather than five years, to complete their degree.

Mentoring

Numerous studies of the effects of mentoring have been published (Faison 1996; 1993). Since mentoring focuses on increasing retention and success, these studies clearly track the effects of mentoring on such outcome measures, often reporting remarkable differences between participants and non-participants. The reports on mentoring show that it works for both undergraduate and graduate students as the recipients of mentoring and when both faculty and peers serve as mentors. Astin (1984) and Tinto (1987) have demonstrated that campus involvement and social integration correlate with heightened levels of academic persistence and achievement. It is likely that mentoring succeeds because it contributes to students' experience of involvement and support within the campus community

Wilson (1994) reports on a freshman mentoring program at a community college in rural Georgia. At the end of one quarter, the author found that the mentoring program helped retain eighty-eight percent of the participating students, as compared with an overall retention rate of fifty-three percent for students who lacked mentors. Terrell and Hassell (1994) also discuss results of research on successful mentoring programs. Most programs had a combination of faculty, staff, peers, and others, such as alumni/ae mentoring students. Retention rates ranged from sixty-four to ninety-eight percent. Three institutions reported a seventy-five percent retention rate and two institutions achieved a ninety percent retention rate. One mentoring program helped retain ninety-two percent of the participants, while only sixty-two percent of the students that did not participate in mentoring remained at the end of the second term.

Several studies concentrate on the effects of peer mentors on retention. Guon (1988) studied the effects of peer counselors who provided academic tutoring, social support, and positive social role modeling across three groups: at-risk minority students participating in the program, non-minority students not in the program, and at-risk minority students not in the program. Multiple regression analysis reveals that program membership, followed by first-term grade point average, are the strongest predictors of year-end enrollment status. Eighty two percent of the program students were retained as compared to seventy-four percent of the non-program students. Bell and Drakeford (1992) examine the efficacy of an African American student peer mentor program for first year students. Results indicate that participants in the mentor program were significantly less likely than those in the control group to drop out of the institution. All participants returned to the institution for their sophomore year. Peer mentor participants were also more likely than non-participants to become involved in campus organizations and activities. Overall, the peer mentor program helped its participants feel more connected to the university. Fuertes, Cothran, and Sedlacek (1991) similarly present a model of the importance of Latino/a student involvement in a mentoring program to aid student retention.

Along with mentoring programs that include peer involvement, there are studies that specifically discuss the need for and benefits of faculty involvement in mentoring (Adams and Wadsworth 1989; Hurtado, Carter, and Spuler 1996; Tate and Schwartz 1993). Still other articles report comparable praise and results for the efficacy of both kinds of mentoring to curb student attrition (Abdullahi 1992; Minner, et al. 1995; Wenzlaff and Biewer 1996).

The value of mentoring for women of color has also been reported. Nora, Hagedorn, Cabrera, and Pascarella (1994) studied twenty-six two-year and four-year, private and public, commuter and residential colleges to examine the cognitive, affective, and environmental factors that influenced persistence. Results indicate that academic achievement and persistence are strongly related to each other, and suggest that tutoring, study groups, and academic counseling seem the most useful interventions to support both. For minority students, dropping out is strongly associated with family responsibilities and working off campus, factors which are not negated by strong peer and faculty relationships or academic experiences. For women, however, including women of color, faculty mentoring and non-classroom interaction with faculty prove to have a significant positive impact on persistence.

A report of equivocal results of mentoring programs comes from Johnson and Sullivan (1995), who review the literature on mentoring programs for pre-service teachers. They do find that one-to-one mentoring and meeting with students once a week is key. Even with this outcome and Nora, Hagedorn, Cabrera, and Pascarella's (1994) finding that strong peer and faculty relationships cannot entirely overcome the impact of family and work responsibilities on minority student retention, faculty and peer mentoring programs appear worthwhile.

Although initial participation in higher education and persistence to the degree are improving for traditionally underrepresented groups, both access and persistence remain areas of concern. Moreover, higher education is behind in documenting access and success for new immigrant groups and others. However, a number of successful approaches have been identified. These approaches share an emphasis on collaborative, community efforts that involve students working with peers and/or faculty in on-going activities such as mentoring, tutoring, or community involvement which emphasize that the students have the academic and social abilities to succeed in college and to meet high expectations. These approaches, when combined with such institutional support factors as financial aid, honors programs, transition to college support programs, and an institutional belief in the students, have proven successful. One lesson that stands out from the review of this research is that the most successful programs are those that combine several methods in a coherent approach which also takes into account students' family and cultural contexts.

Those methods that have proven most responsive to student needs are ones that have stressed the need for institutional structures and programs to be changed or designed to meet the needs of new students. Campuses cannot expect to be successful in retaining new students if the institutional status quo remains. In many cases, successful retention efforts have called for innovation and restructuring of more traditional programs and approaches.

4

Campus Climate and Intergroup Relations

The campus climate is the environment of the college or university. This environment can itself have significant impact on students' access, retention and academic success. Efforts to address issues of climate on campus have emerged, in part, from a large body of research which reports nearly universal experiences of difficulty with the prevailing institutional cultures among specific groups of students. We address these issues and their implications for campus diversity in this chapter.

Interaction among students, another subject of considerable attention on campus and elsewhere, also is addressed in this chapter. There has been much discussion in recent years about both the actual and the desirable state of relations and interactions among diverse student groups. Some point to the need for non-majority students to have comfortable secure spaces in which they can spend part of their time with others who share their identifications. Such spaces, it is argued, free students from the unremitting pressures of interacting at all times as members of a minority group. Others, often critical of any attention to diversity issues, suggest that programs supporting particular communal identities fragment the larger campus community. They argue that higher education should transcend rather than acknowledge significant and historically inherited societal differences. Yet a third group contends that campuses should support both strong affiliations and strong intergroup connections. Research supporting this third position is discussed later in this chapter.

The literature dealing with campus climate is extensive. We organize the literature on this subject around evidence of campus climate difficulties, strategies which contribute to an improved climate and academic success, and research on intergroup relations.

Evidence of Campus Climate Difficulty

The literature on campus climate and its *negative* effects on minority student populations centers on nearly universal reports of feelings of alienation, hostility, and difficulties fitting in to prevailing institutional cultures. Students report language barriers (Minner, et al. 1995), problems with the campus environment (Chan and Wang 1991; Kibble, Malmberg, and Ratwik 1990), difficulties with acculturation (Tate and Schwartz 1993), social isolation (Bennett and Okinaka 1990), invisibility (Osajima 1995), and outright hostility (D'Augelli 1992; Herek 1993; LaSalle and Rhoads 1992; Nettles 1990a; Turner 1994).

These feelings have a negative impact on students' sense of belonging and retention in college (Hurtado and Carter 1994), impair academic adjustment (LeSure 1993), lower overall campus life satisfaction (D'Augelli and Hershberger 1993), affect grades (Fuertes and Sedlacek 1995), and decrease graduation rates (Tafalla, Rivera, and Tuchel 1993). The negative impact of discrimination and feelings of isolation are clear. How can institutions create environments that compensate for this alienation? Several studies report successful methods.

Support Services, Programs, and Centers

Building on Tinto's (1987) concept of social integration as a major factor in student retention, a number of studies have pointed to the significance of involvement in ethnic student support groups and other groups on campus. Hurtado and Carter's 1994 study of Latino/a students examines the influence of factors related to persistence. Results show that those students belonging to a variety of college organizations increased adjustment and attachment to the institution. Gilliard (1996) and Hurtado, Dey and Treviño (1994) found positive benefits of participation in racial and ethnic groups and that these groups fostered intergroup contact. Fuertes, Cothran, and Sedlacek (1991) confirm the importance of involvement in campus activities in general in aiding student retention of Latino/a students. The value of general involvement in campus activities and organizations is clear.

As services specifically designed to support minority students, racial and ethnic student theme houses, student organizations, and academic departments appear to positively contribute to minority student retention, despite widespread challenges based on their assumed negative effect on the development of inclusive campus community. Wright (1990) found a significant relationship between attendance at American Indian student organization meetings and the retention of American Indian students. Spitzburg and Thorndike (1992) conducted a study of African American alumni who participated in theme houses. They suggest that students' experiences were positive in contrast to those who only lived in predominantly white residential settings. Likewise, Lomotey (1990b) found that an African American theme house provided support and cultural enrichment, an African American student organization added political advantage,

SERVICES SPECIFICALLY DESIGNED TO SUPPORT MINORITY STUDENTS, RACIAL AND ETHNIC STUDENT THEME HOUSES, STUDENT ORGANIZATIONS, AND ACADEMIC DEPARTMENTS APPEAR TO POSITIVELY CONTRIBUTE TO MINORITY STUDENT RETENTION.

and the African American Studies department added status for these students. Lomotey (1990a) also reports the importance of vigilance in ensuring the success of African American students, the need for students to rely on one another, the importance of a critical mass of African American students on a predominantly white campus, and the need to hire, reward, and retain African American faculty and staff.

Again bridging the gap between academic and co-curricular sources of support, Falk and Aitken (1984) report American Indian Studies programs as important or very important in improving American Indian retention. Wright's report (1990) also found that American Indian Studies programs provide support services to American Indian students that improve retention. Kibble, Malmberg, and Ratwik's (1990) study of American Indian graduates finds family housing and the campus American Indian center as sources of support. From these reports, it appears that programs and organizations designed to aid underrepresented students increase their likelihood of persistence.

Trippi and Cheatham (1989) also found a special counseling program to be positively related to African American students' persistence in college and their degree status. The efficacy of support services is not universal, however. Livingston and Steward report that African American students have long resisted support services at predominantly white institutions (1987). Accordingly, African American non-persisters have been found to make less use of campus services (Kibble, Malmberg, and Ratwik 1990). This research echos Cross's (1974) landmark review of the characteristics of students "new" to higher education. This review demonstrated that majority *and* minority students alike often failed to seek academic help or to use support services until it was too late. A reconceptualization of student services and their access and delivery to many student groups may be needed at institutions that have students who show this pattern. Overall, however, the pattern of the research which is emerging suggests strongly that involvement in specialized student groups, such as ethnic theme houses, benefits students of color and others who choose to participate.

> THE PATTERN OF THE RESEARCH WHICH IS EMERGING SUGGESTS STRONGLY THAT INVOLVEMENT IN SPECIALIZED STUDENT GROUPS, SUCH AS ETHNIC THEME HOUSES, BENEFITS STUDENTS OF COLOR AND OTHERS WHO CHOOSE TO PARTICIPATE.

Intergroup Relations

The research on the relationships among groups of college students is developing particularly in response to questions about the best approaches to fostering interaction and continuing concerns about the many barriers to interaction on campus. The research presented here ranges in scope. Some of the studies draw from large national data bases. Some are longitudinal in nature while others have been conducted to measure the efficacy of a particular program, training, or experience on a more limited number of students in a specific campus setting.

Astin (1993) uses data from the Higher Education Research Institute to examine several issues including the effect of direct involvement in diversity experiences on academic progress and values. After controlling for entering student characteristics, he reports that interaction with others from different cultures is associated with positive outcomes including cultural awareness and overall satisfaction with college. Antony (1993), addressing the extent to which college affects students' sense of the importance of promoting racial understanding, found this attitude to be mediated by many variables that are independent of students' race, or any other background characteristics, and almost entirely dependent on the sorts of activities and courses students select. These findings strongly support the notion that students' college activities, courses, and involvement are highly predictive of attitude formation toward racial diversity.

Differential impacts of types of involvement were also found by Pascarella, Edison, Nora, Hagedorn, and Terenzini's (1996) study which sought to determine the factors influencing students' openness to diversity and challenge during the first year of college. It focused particularly on white students. Controlling for student background characteristics and other confounding influences, a non-discriminatory racial environment, on-campus residence, participation in a racial or cultural awareness workshop, and a large degree of involvement with diverse peers had positive effects on openness to diversity and challenge. Conversely, Greek affiliation for white students had a negative effect. Yet, while Greek affiliation for white students impairs openness to diversity, Greek affiliation in non-white organizations is beneficial for minority students' sense of belonging (Hurtado and Carter 1994).

Colleges' influence on racial attitudes also varies across different groups of students. Hyun (1996) used longitudinal data to examine whether colleges and universities have an impact on students' commitment to promote racial understanding. This study found that African American students' commitment to racial understanding increased at a greater rate than the commitment of white students, but that there was a positive effect for both groups. Lopez (1993) used a sample of first-year students to investigate the impact of intergroup contact and course work on students' approaches to dealing with racial and ethnic issues. The results of intergroup contact were mixed, with white students showing increased support for equity issues after contact. This was not as true for African American students. Chen (1995) found benefits to the experience of classroom diversity in an Asian American studies course, although there was a negative impact on Asian American students' participation when classes became predominantly white. Yet the desire for interaction remains, as reported by Fischer and Hartmann's (1995) findings that sixty-one percent of whites and sixty-seven percent of African Americans on a predominantly white campus requested more opportunities involving interracial interaction, communication, and activities.

Several researchers have published evaluations of programs designed to promote intergroup contact and understanding (Guarasci and Cornwell 1997; Schoem 1996; Zúñiga, Vasques, Sevig, and Nagda n.d.). For example, Zúñiga,

Nagda, Sevig, Thompson, and Dey (1995) conducted a series of studies of students at the University of Michigan who participated in an intergroup dialogue program. They found that the intergroup dialogues were effective in decreasing prejudicial attitudes. Nelson, Johnson, Boyd, and Scott (1994) similarly evaluated the impact of a program designed to facilitate communication and understanding among college students from diverse backgrounds. Results suggest that white students were more optimistic about intergroup understanding, more comfortable interacting with minority students, and more aware of racial issues after participating in the group.

Maluso (1992) compared two strategies—the impact of exposure to either a high status minority group member or participation in a cultural diversity workshop—on entering white students during a new student orientation program. Twelve weeks after orientation, students were given several tests to determine the impact of the various strategies. Interaction with the high status minority group member had a positive impact on later selection of a person of color in a photo choice task. Again, intergroup contact appears to positively influence students.

> COLLEGE PROVIDES NEW OPPORTUNITIES FOR STUDENTS TO DEVELOP AN UNDERSTANDING OF SEXUAL DIVERSITY AND CONTACT WITH A BISEXUAL, GAY, OR LESBIAN PERSON IS THE PRIMARY CATALYST FOR ATTITUDE CHANGE.

While most studies have had race and racial attitudes as their focus, some studies have also been done that focus on other marginalized student groups. These studies are often focused on a particular educational method or a particular campus. Several studies have reported results of educational programs geared to improving the institutional climate or the overall effect of the college experience on student attitudes toward lesbians, gays, and bisexuals (University of Wisconsin-Stevens Point 1992; Watanabe 1992). Croteau and Kusek's (1992) definitive research review on the universal success of gay and lesbian speaker panels gathers available literature on the use of interpersonal contact with lesbians and gays to decrease prejudicial attitudes. Kardia's (1996) study finds that college provides new opportunities for students to develop an understanding of sexual diversity and that contact with a bisexual, gay, or lesbian person is the primary catalyst for attitude change.

Similar benefits have been found for contact with international students. Sharma and Mulka (1993) researched the impact of international education upon United States students. Results indicate that the higher the interaction level with international students, the more positive the attitudes of U.S. students.

The effects of a diverse student body on intergroup relations have also been examined. Hurtado, Dey, and Treviño (1994), in one study explicitly investigating self-segregation, used 1987 Higher Education Research Institute freshman and 1991 follow-up data to examine patterns of intergroup contact on campuses across the country. Results confirm that self-segregation is not a general pattern among students of color and that ethnic specific activities for these students does not impede interracial contact. White students clearly had fewer interactions across groups. The results suggest that structured opportunities in classes and in organizations were positively related to the level of intergroup interactions.

Chang (1996) examined whether a racially mixed student population affected educational outcomes. Looking at 11,000 students on 300 campuses, Chang quantified the racial diversity at each institution, measuring opportunities for cross-racial interaction. Findings are that environmental and experiential components of a diverse campus have positive affects on retention, overall college satisfaction, college grade point average, and intellectual and social self-confidence.

We noted above the divide between those who, citing the research, emphasize the importance of strong group affiliation and support in fostering student success and those who fear the fragmenting effects of identity programs on campus community. In this context, there is encouragement to be found in a large ethnographic study of students on issues of diversity and multiculturalism (Duster, 1995; Institute for the Study of Social Change 1995 reprint).

Troy Duster and his colleagues report that there is both a trend toward strong group affiliations and also significant student interest in experiencing greater levels of interaction across groups at Berkeley. The group affiliations, Duster reports, help students negotiate a complex social experience on campus. They also provide students with opportunities to probe the substantial diversity *within* groups that outsiders may view as homogeneous. At the same time, the study shows that, in general, students anticipate and desire greater levels of intergroup contact than they actually experience at Berkeley. Students who reported positive intergroup interactions found them in cooperative learning situations where students worked together in classes and in group projects. Taken together, these findings lead Duster to conclude that the faculty need to take active responsibility for creating enhanced classroom opportunities for students to benefit from interaction across groups.

> ENVIRONMENTAL AND EXPERIENTIAL COMPONENTS OF A DIVERSE CAMPUS HAVE POSITIVE AFFECTS ON RETENTION, OVERALL COLLEGE SATISFACTION, COLLEGE GRADE POINT AVERAGE, AND INTELLECTUAL AND SOCIAL SELF-CONFIDENCE.

These studies provide a valuable lens through which to interpret the diverse findings we report in this chapter. Students of color clearly benefit positively from the presence of those who are like them in academic and social settings. Yet many also value intergroup connections as well. Majority students benefit from their interactions with students who are different from themselves. This research is beginning to suggest a new path—one that might encourage students to benefit from affiliation and interaction with those who are like and those who are different. This path also reinforces the notion that students have multiple identifications which can be developed. Participating in support groups does not negate the many other opportunities for interaction.

Through the sweep of this literature on the effects of programs and environments promoting intergroup relations, the research rather clearly confirms the efficacy of opportunities for interaction among student groups and their positive outcomes on a variety of educational, attitudinal, and affective measures. Many of these approaches are based on long-standing intergroup relations research which suggests that the *context* for effective individual interactions requires institutional support, equal status, and common goals (e.g. Pettigrew 1994).

This chapter has focused on three critical areas concerning campus climate: 1) the experience of a campus climate or culture by groups of students; 2) the institutional and programmatic strategies that have proved effective in improving campus climate for both majority and non-majority students; and 3) the current research on student intergroup interactions and social relations. The research clearly documents that students of color and others often find the campus climate unresponsive to their needs, past experiences, and educational expectations. Students often feel marginalized in existing institutional cultures and the various effects of that marginalization (feelings of alienation, lack of attention to a diversity of cultures within the curriculum or in campus extracurricular programming, or overt acts of prejudice) have a strong effect on both the retention of current students and the recruitment of new students.

At the same time, one persistent research finding is the fact that student involvement with campus groups that reflect personal, cultural, or service interests have a strong impact on helping students feel that they belong on the campus, are contributing to the campus culture, and have their interests reflected in the institutional structure. As we saw in the previous chapter, student involvement in academic and social groups is a key factor in building community and fostering opportunity to develop more empathic attitudes toward individual differences and to learn from a diverse group of faculty and peers.

INDIVIDUAL GROUP CONTACT OVER TIME ALLOWS STUDENTS TO BREAK DOWN STEREOTYPES AND TO BECOME MORE REFLECTIVE OF THEIR OWN AND OTHERS' EXPERIENCES AND PERSPECTIVES

The process of intergroup interaction is, however, a most complex and difficult one to study, especially when the very students who strongly indicate the desire for intercultural contact often differ in the meaning of that contact (Duster 1995). And while the studies cited above vary, the data seems to indicate that individual group contact over time allows students to break down stereotypes and to become more reflective of their own and others' experiences and perspectives—and that this has a positive effect on both the students' perception of college and their learning.

5

Education and Scholarship: Curriculum, Teaching, and Learning

The third dimension of our diversity framework examines the educational and scholarly work of the academy. The literature reviewed in this section ranges from broad findings on the inclusion of multicultural material in course work, through evaluations of diversity courses, women's studies classes, and cultural awareness programs, to measures of the effects of differing pedagogical strategies. Perhaps the most significant shift observable in this literature has been the judgment that changes in curriculum and pedagogy are needed not just to "satisfy" certain groups of new students. Rather, these changes are needed to fulfill institutional and societal concerns about preparing all students for a pluralistic society and world.

A recent review and summary of campus approaches to bringing diversity into the curriculum (Humphreys and Schneider 1997) demonstrates the broad range of approaches to curricular development and change being implemented by colleges and universities. Some examples of new directions are: changes from courses narrowly focused on identity to courses focusing on the practices that gave rise to exclusion of groups that are different; expansion of the categories of diversity beyond those of gender and race/ethnicity to include age, disability, religion, and sexual orientation; approaches that are more comparative and cross-cultural; and the growth in approaches that educate for social responsibility by focusing on relationships, experiences, and problem-solving across groups. Experiential education activities like service-learning often fit this model as well. More detailed discussions of specific models are available on Diversity Web (http://www.inform.umd.edu/diversityweb). We discuss some examples of research in what has worked in this area in the following pages.

Diversity in the Curriculum

Only a few years ago, Francis (1993) asserted that there was little but anecdotal and descriptive evidence available to demonstrate the effectiveness of multicultural curriculum initiatives. That situation has changed. Astin (1993) used a national longitudinal study to examine the effect of multiple diversity experiences on student attitudes and behaviors, and the effect of direct involvement in diversity experiences on academic progress and values. After controlling for entering student characteristics, Astin finds that faculty emphasis on diversity in courses has positive effects on openness to racial understanding and overall satisfaction with college. Other studies corroborate Astin. Villalpando (1994) looks at the differential impact of diversity initiatives on minority and white students. Students who reported higher levels of satisfaction were those who had faculty who included racial/ethnic materials in their courses. Tanaka (1996) examines the positive impact of multiculturalism on white students' sense of community, cultural awareness, interest in promoting racial understanding, and general satisfaction with college. Inclusion of racial and ethnic material in the curriculum also has positive effects on student outcomes. At the University of Michigan, Lopez (1993) used a sample of first-year students, to investigate the impact of intergroup contact and course work dealing with racial and ethnic issues. While there were some group differences, in general, course work had the most significant positive impact on increased support for educational equity. Duster (Institute for the Study of Social Change 1995) also reports that a multicultural course requirement led students to a greater appreciation of the complexity of cultural production in various cultures. Those students that reported positive interactions found them in cooperative learning situations created in classes and projects. Evidently student satisfaction with college and increased cultural understanding are directly related to the inclusion of multicultural material in the classroom.

> FACULTY EMPHASIS ON DIVERSITY IN COURSES HAS POSITIVE EFFECTS ON STUDENTS' OPENNESS TO RACIAL UNDERSTANDING AND OVERALL SATISFACTION WITH COLLEGE.

Several studies support the contention that cultural diversity courses produce other positive outcomes among students (Hasslen 1993). Adams and Zhou-McGovern (1994) found cognitive development advances among students participating in a course on multiculturalism. Bidell, Lee, Bouchie, Ward, and Brass' (1994) study found that white students enrolled in a college cultural diversity course showed movement in deepening their understandings of the concept of racism.

A number of studies have been published on the effect of multicultural programs and teaching methods specifically in teacher education programs. Sparks and Verner (1993) examine interventions to successfully reduce prejudicial attitudes and increase multicultural knowledge of pre-service teachers. The results indicate that students who were exposed to multicultural education through course work increased their level of racial awareness and understanding of multiple cultures. Moore and Reeves-Kazelskis' (1992) study investigated the extent to which formal instruction on the topic of multicultural education produces changes in white pre-service teachers' beliefs. In this case, formal instruction consisted of lecture and dialogue between two professors of different racial backgrounds. Students did positively change their beliefs and attitudes during the seven weeks of the study. Garmon (1996) also studied the impact of a course in multicultural education on the racial attitudes and beliefs of prospective teachers. The significant finding of the study is that students' initial racial attitudes and beliefs played a major role in mediating the impact of the course. Students who began the course with more positive and favorable racial beliefs were more likely to change in the direction intended than students who began the course with less positive racial attitudes and beliefs.

Other studies have also evaluated the effect of multicultural course content on students, with mixed results. Kayabasi (1988) examines the extent to which students' interest in different cultures are affected by their participation in a World Civilization course. Students in both a control group and those enrolled in the World Civilization course showed a significant increase in interest, self-perceived knowledge, and actual knowledge of different cultures. The author hypothesizes that the diverse nature of the student population may contribute to the students' experiences with cultural diversity and therefore their openness to the issue. While the particular course produced no differences in cultural interest, students' involvement in a diverse environment may have produced the intended results.

Increasing numbers of studies have reported the effects of women's studies courses on students. In a national case study approach assessing the impact of women's studies courses, Musil (1992) finds that women's studies fosters the development of voice, empowerment, and ultimately critical thinking in students, and the sense of empowerment is translated into a greater sense of responsibility for others after graduation. Most importantly, the study finds that women's studies students debate issues far more frequently both in and out of class and gain new insights that help them understand and relate differently to people who are different from themselves. Stake and Gerner (1987) studied the impact of enrolling in an introductory women's studies course for both male and female students. Both men and women in women's studies courses demonstrated greater gains in self-esteem, job motivation, and job certainty when compared to a control group. Bargad and Hyde (1991) found that women's studies courses had positive influences on women students' sense of feminist identity. Pence (1992) designed a study to measure how women's attitudes toward men differ among those enrolled in an introductory women's studies course and those enrolled in an introductory sociology course. The results of the study indicate that attitudes toward men improved for the women in the women's studies course. Based on the data, the author concludes that women's studies courses are falsely perceived as hostile towards men and may, in fact, help women to better understand and appreciate men.

WOMEN'S STUDIES STUDENTS DEBATE ISSUES FAR MORE FREQUENTLY BOTH IN AND OUT OF CLASS AND GAIN NEW INSIGHTS THAT HELP THEM UNDERSTAND AND RELATE DIFFERENTLY TO PEOPLE WHO ARE DIFFERENT FROM THEMSELVES.

A series of studies using the federally-funded National Study of Student Learning have reported on the sometimes contentious issue of the effectiveness of racial or cultural awareness workshops. Some educators argue that these programs increase racial sensitivity and tolerance. Others suggest they may heighten awareness of racial differences (Nesbitt, et al. 1994). However, Pascarella, Whitt, Nora, Edison, Hagedorn, and Terenzini (1996), controlling for student background characteristics, indicate that racial or cultural awareness workshops foster students' openness to cultural, racial, and value diversity.

Delving further into aspects of the National Study of Student Learning, Springer, Palmer, Terenzini, Pascarella, and Nora (1996) assessed the effects of awareness programs on the attitudes of white students towards diversity on campus. The study found that students who stayed in particular majors, like business or economics, during the first two years of college were significantly less likely to participate in racial or cultural awareness work-shops than students in other liberal arts fields. These authors also conclude that taking awareness workshops positively influences student attitudes toward diversity on campus.

Guarasci (1997) describes a service-learning project that is a form of experiential education at a small liberal arts college. The program includes both a classroom and a field study component that involves the community in the educational process and fosters responsibility and citizenship in a diverse world. Analysis of student essays demonstrates the positive impact of this type of service-learning program. The uses of service-learning within women's studies curricula are reviewed by Trigg and Balliet (1997). Their review of student essays reveals the role that service-learning activities play in developing student awareness of and sensitivity to multiple aspects of diversity.

Teaching Strategies

A variety of pedagogical methods for multicultural education have been studied. Ortíz (1995), in an interesting study emphasizing differentiated teaching strategies, finds that informal peer interaction and peer-led discussions in class are effective for all students, but especially for first year students who prefer this as their primary vehicle for learning about multicultural issues. Fourth year students found that instructor-led discussions and activities were most effective for them and they supported and preferred instructors playing a large role in the learning agenda. Required and supplemental readings were also found to be highly effective in promoting racial understanding in these students. The results of this study also show students with prior experiences with discrimination and racism have much higher expectations for educational interventions, trainers and instructors. These students found their peers were better sources of information than instructors or trainers.

Hasslen (1993) reports that pairing white students with students of color lessens myths and reduces fear of difference. Benns-Suter (1993) finds the use of simulation methods to be effective in stimulating thinking about multicultural issues. Grant and Secada (1990), reviewing many studies which assessed the effect of multicultural education, found the most effective strategies involve intense exposure to diversity issues. Further, the more time spent learning the content, the more varied the presentation, and the more course work covers these issues, the more likely learning will be successful. Each of these studies points toward the effectiveness of increasing personal and interpersonal involvement with pluralism to deepen its educational and affective impact.

Powers (1996) examines the impact of a hypermedia-based computer program on knowledge and awareness of multicultural issues and on student interactions. The program was applied to three groups of undergraduate students in three different ways: individually, in pairs, and in facilitated discussions. Of the three possible methods, the facilitated discussion had the greatest impact on students' knowledge and awareness. Again, personal involvement with peers and the instructor, in conjunction with media, was the most effective.

The literature on changing students' negative attitudes toward lesbians, gays, and bisexuals echoes the effectiveness of intergroup relations and students' involvement across difference in affecting change. The most active and promising area of research has been on lesbian and gay panel presentations with question and answer periods, which Croteau and Kusek (1992) analyzed. They found that such forums succeeded in reducing prejudicial attitudes. Several other studies have been published confirming these results (Geasler, Croteau, Heineman, and Edlund 1995; Green, Dixon, and Gold-Neil 1993; Nelson and Krieger 1997; Curtis and Heritage 1991).

Two recent publications have evaluated the effects of differing representations of lesbians and gays to measure their impact on students' attitudes. Corley and Pollack (1996) measured the effect of stereotypical descriptions of a lesbian couple. Men with higher traditional sex role values showed significantly more positive attitudes toward lesbians after they read a non-stereotypical description of the lesbian couple. Piskur and Degelman (1992) investigated if attitudes toward homosexuals change when the reading material suggests there is a biological basis to homosexuality. They found that among women, the biological explanation seemed to engender a positive attitude toward homosexuals. Marchesani (1994) similarly used science fiction reading material to increase awareness of lesbian and gay issues. Contrary to the almost uniform findings of success in this research, an abnormally high number of students immediately quit the class. The professor also received the lowest student course ratings for any course he had taught when he focused the entire syllabus on readings that depicted alternative sexualities as ordinary.

While we did not conduct an extensive search of the literature on disabilities, a few studies we discovered address the issue of students with learning disabilities (Gobbo and Bolaski 1997; Keim, McWhirter, and Berstein 1996). Those that we include are uniform in their findings that institutional and instructor accommodations compensate for entering lags in achievement and subsequent test performance. Runyan (1991) measured the performance of students with learning disabilities compared to normally achieving students on tests of reading comprehension and reading rates. Under timed conditions, students with learning disabilities achieved significantly lower scores than the normally achieving group. Yet, when each group was given extra time, no differences in performance appeared. Normally achieving students did not perform significantly better with extra time.

Other studies examine the impact of technology and media in multicultural education. Childers (1997) reports results of a project funded by the Institute for Public Media Arts in which a video documentary production helps students become reflective about their attitudes toward diversity and in the process create public dialogue to improve student relations. Some of the positive outcomes of the project include interest between cultures generated by video diaries, the ability of students to speak more openly about their experiences and reservations, and the opportunity to learn about each other in a personal and academic setting. Videos and slide presentations have also been used with success to increase acceptance of sexual diversity (Beckham-Chasnoff 1996; Walters 1994).

There is, then, a significant body of literature which suggests that serious engagement of diversity in the curriculum, along with linking classroom and out-of-class opportunities, positively affect students' attitudes and awareness about diversity, as well as their commitment to education, and their involvement. The research also shows connections between taking such courses and increased satisfaction with college. The classroom appears to be a powerful location for intergroup dialogue and learning. These benefits seem most apparent for white students, in part because they tend to have notably *less* opportunity for such engagement. At the same time, the impact such efforts have on the climate and on the education of students from diverse backgrounds is also emerging as important and positive.

THE CLASSROOM APPEARS TO BE A POWERFUL LOCATION FOR INTERGROUP DIALOGUE AND LEARNING.

The past two decades of work in the parallel areas of curriculum transformation and pedagogical innovation in higher education have produced a rich variety of curricular and pedagogical models that have been tailored to the specific missions and educational goals of particular campuses. It is beyond the scope of this chapter to review all that literature. Instead, we have focused on recent findings about the effect of the curriculum and new teaching methods on knowledge, attitudes, and intellectual capacities with respect to intercultural awareness and understanding.

The research indicates that there have been a broad range of curricular approaches that include multicultural perspectives. Whether the approach is one that is campus-wide, one that is included in the general education requirements, or one that is more extra-curricular, the results seem to be consistent: 1) The inclusion of cultural diversity content and perspectives in coursework has positive effects on critical thinking skills and knowledge acquisition, 2) Faculty involvement plays a key role in students acquiring more empathic and complex ways of thinking about difference and in reducing bias against particular individuals or groups; 3) Co-curricular educational programs are also effective in creating awareness and reducing prejudice, but are more effective if conducted on campuses that have such an emphasis in the curriculum as well; and 4) Pedagogical approaches that involve students working together across differences and on a common learning goal are also effective. Such approaches as cooperative learning, service learning and collaborative learning communities have a strong record of facilitating intellectual complexity and multicultural competencies.

COLLABORATIVE LEARNING COMMUNITIES HAVE A STRONG RECORD OF FACILITATING INTELLECTUAL COMPLEXITY AND MULTICULTURAL COMPETENCIES.

6

Institutional Transformation: Findings on Comprehensive Campus Commitments to Diversity

The fourth dimension in our analysis of campus diversity efforts addresses comprehensive institutional commitments to diversity and their effects on students. We include in this category the role of visible leadership, mission statements, faculty and staff diversity and students' own self-reported perceptions that diversity is taken seriously on campus.

Comprehensive commitment to the value and significance of campus diversity is a key, the research suggests, to the effectiveness of diversity initiatives. This commitment must pervade the institution from senior administrators through faculty and staff; it must be both communicated and demonstrated to students. It cannot be solely the work of the student affairs staff, a small group of faculty, or those who are directly served by diversity programs. Students have alert antennae that readily distinguish between lip service and pervasive values. Throughout the research literature, we have uncovered consistent, positive outcomes for students who perceive that their campus has made a strong commitment to the value of diversity. In this chapter we examine this emerging evidence.

The Effect of Institutional Commitment to Diversity

In Astin's (1993) groundbreaking, multi-institutional study of the impact of diversity on students, he examines how students' academic progress, values and beliefs are affected after four years of college by institutional policies and practices related to diversity. After controlling for entering student characteristics, Astin found that students' perception of an institutional commitment to diversity is strongly associated with their overall satisfaction with college.

Villalpando (1994) also reports that an institution's commitment to a strong multicultural environment had a significant impact on student satisfaction regardless of the student's background. Smith, Wolf, and Morrison (1995) similarly found that institutional commitment to diversity contributes to the satisfaction and success of all students, both of which are central to the goals of higher education.

Institutional commitment to diversity also affects how students plan to engage with diversity issues after college. In a four-year longitudinal study, Astin (1993) also found association between institutional diversity policies and practices and the development of student cultural awareness and commitment to promoting racial understanding. In another broad national study, Pascarella, Whitt, Nora, Edison, Hagedorn, and Terenzini (1996) indicate that openness to diversity was also positively influenced by a nondiscriminatory racial environment.

Gilliard (1996) studied the impact of campus racial climate on the success of African American and white students on six predominantly white Midwestern colleges and universities. The study concludes that an institutional climate that supports and affirms people from racially and ethnically diverse backgrounds is important for the success of all students. Tanaka (1996) examined the impact of multiculturalism, and found that institutional efforts to create a multicultural environment and inclusion of racial and ethnic material in the curriculum have positive effects on white students' sense of community, cultural awareness, interest in promoting racial understanding, and general satisfaction with college.

STUDENTS' PERCEPTION OF AN INSTITUTIONAL COMMITMENT TO DIVERSITY IS STRONGLY ASSOCIATED WITH THEIR OVERALL SATISFACTION WITH COLLEGE.

From this variety of studies using student outcomes from many institutions, one may conclude that an institutional emphasis on creating a strong multicultural educational environment has positive effects on students' satisfaction with college, cultural awareness, and commitment to promoting racial understanding, regardless of student background or entering characteristics. As the most sweeping confirmation of the effect of diversity on campuses, one may argue that diversity does work.

Special Purpose Institutions as Models of Commitment

This group of studies includes research on the impact of institutions which move marginalized students to the center. The literature on special purpose institutions—historically black colleges and universities (HBCUs), women's colleges, American Indian colleges, and Latino/a serving institutions, lays bare the debate over self-segregation, intergroup contact, and who benefits by diversity. Often diversity initiatives in predominantly white, male-focused institutions seem clearly to benefit white students who have experience with and are comfortable within that environment. Institutions which reverse this population, institutional focus, and power dynamic have definite benefits for the students they serve. Baccalaureate origin studies habitually show the benefit of these special mission institutions for their students who are more likely to attain the Ph.D. or pursue non-traditional careers in science and mathematics (Solorzano 1995; Wolf 1995). Significant factors in the success of these institutions include their high expectations of their students and their levels of support for students.

Several studies examine student experiences in HBCUs. Watson and Kuh (1996) examined the relationship between involvement in campus activities, perceptions of the institutional environment, and educational gains of undergraduates at two predominantly black and two predominantly white liberal arts institutions. African American students at the HBCUs benefited more from their overall involvement compared with white students and with African American students at predominantly white institutions. Nottingham, Rosen, and Parks' (1992) study, however, found no difference in several aspects of psychological well-being between African American students at an HBCU and at a predominantly white institution.

Fleming's (1985) book presents the results of a major study of the experience of African American students on white campuses and HBCUs. The study looks at student experiences in terms of achievement, cognitive development, and student backgrounds. Her results present evidence of the importance of campus climate, involvement in campus life, interaction with faculty, and expectations for success. These conditions were more likely to be found at the HBCUs.

HBCUs provide benefits for their students. Davis (1994) finds that African American males attending HBCUs reported significantly higher grade point averages,

STUDENTS AT HBCUS WERE FOUND TO HAVE HIGHER ASPIRATIONS, BETTER ACADEMIC ACHIEVEMENT AS MEASURED BY GRADE POINT AVERAGE, AND A HIGHER LEVEL OF SOCIAL INVOLVEMENT WITH THE CAMPUS RELATIVE TO THEIR COUNTERPARTS AT PREDOMINANTLY WHITE INSTITUTIONS.

were more integrated into the academic life on campus, and perceived their colleges as providing more institutional support than their peers at predominantly white institutions. African Americans attending predominantly white institutions, though, had better study habits. Allen (1992) reports the findings of a survey of African American students at six predominantly white institutions and eight HBCUs. Students at HBCUs were found to have higher aspirations, better academic achievement as measured by grade point average, and a higher level of social involvement with the campus relative to their counterparts at predominantly white institutions. The author stresses the need to understand the reasons behind HBCUs' success with African American students in order to translate it to other types of institutions.

Wolf (1995) demonstrates that special-focus institutions, including HBCUs, women's colleges, and Latino/a serving institutions, graduate a greater proportion of successful women, particularly for the groups each serves, as compared to predominantly white coeducational institutions. The qualitative analysis of the six sample institutions indicates that high academic expectations and support were common factors across the institutions. Other contributors to student success included the presence of role models, the importance of community service, and the power of a focused institutional mission.

The research on women's colleges and their benefits for students is generally consistent with the literature on HBCUs. Baccalaureate origin studies on women began with Tidball's (1980) groundbreaking work showing that graduates of women's colleges are consistently more productive in terms of leadership and doctoral attainment than women graduates from other institutions. Wolf (1995) augmented these findings by disaggregating the data for African American, Latina, and white women and showing the significance of women's colleges and other special purpose institutions. A recent summary by the Department of Education (Harwarth, Maline, and DeBra 1997) summarizes these studies and more.

Riordan (1992) traced the outcomes of women who attended or graduated from women's colleges compared to an equivalent sample of women from mixed-gender colleges. After controls, students who attended at least two years at women's colleges attained significantly higher occupational prestige than women at mixed-gender colleges. The results were mixed for post-baccalaureate educational attainment. Smith (1990) compared responses of women who attended women's colleges and women who attended coeducational colleges on the degree to which they perceived they had changed over four years, their satisfaction with the institution, their educational aspirations, and their perception of institutional goals and values. Analysis suggests that women who attended women's colleges rated their institutions more positively on measures of academic programs and contact with faculty and administration, as well as perceived changes in values of tolerance and cultural awareness. Persistence to graduation was also higher. Social life was rated lower. In an effort to understand the reasons for the success of women's colleges, Smith, Wolf, and Morrison (1995) looked at the institutional factors contributing to success and found that institutional commitment to diversity, to students, and to involvement were significantly related to success.

> STUDENTS WHO ATTENDED AT LEAST TWO YEARS AT WOMEN'S COLLEGES ATTAINED SIGNIFICANTLY HIGHER OCCUPATIONAL PRESTIGE THAN WOMEN AT MIXED-GENDER COLLEGES.

American Indian students also find benefit in tribally controlled colleges. At special purpose institutions, the transformational aspect of diversity is all-encompassing. As noted previously, Belgarde (1992), Boyer (1997), and the Carnegie Foundation for the Advancement of Teaching (1989) have presented the advantages of American Indian-serving institutions. Boyer particularly emphasizes that they establish a learning environment which encourages participation and builds the self-confidence of students who expect to fail. Wright and Head (1990) conducted probably our best example of research into the specific benefits for American Indians who attend a tribally controlled community college. They surveyed all associate degree recipients between 1976 and 1987 from Montana's seven tribal colleges. Nearly two-thirds reported they were employed, with over 10 percent unemployed. Of the remaining people, almost half were full-time students. With Montana's unemployment rate for American Indians at 51 percent, Wright and Head suggest an associate's degree from a tribal college significantly improved students' employment opportunities. These students were also overwhelmingly satisfied with their tribal college experience.

The evidence from these institutions continues to be a powerful lesson for setting high expectations, creating locations which are committed to students, remaining learning centered, providing many models of success, and linking educational success to larger civic goals. Such institutions offer strategies for student success that could provide models for other schools. It should be emphasized, however, that at this time there is a lack of research that demonstrates how these campuses have attempted to educate their students with respect to the broad range of racial, ethnic, class, gender, sexual orientation, and ability groups that represent other forms of diversity.

Implementing Institutional Commitments to Diversity

The question then becomes, "How does one make diversity operational at the institutional level?" Numerous factors have been cited as integral to organizational change to achieve a pluralistic college or university. Heading the list are leadership, mission, faculty and staff diversity, and overall institutional commitment to the goal.

Bensimon (1995) examines the efforts of a university to transform an organizational structure that is monocultural to one that is grounded in the diversity of the student body. Results of her case study indicate that leadership was crucial to the institution's transformation, that a new mission statement had a significant effect, as did the appointment of women and minority group members to the president's cabinet. Other factors affecting the institution's transformation were the appointment of African Americans and Latino/a's to the faculty, and multicultural curricular transformation. The Education Commission of the States (1990) similarly reports that approaching the issue of student diversity from the perspective of organizational culture can help institutional leaders avoid the pursuit of strategies that promise diminishing returns. Like Bensimon, Varlotta (1997) makes the case for the use of the institution's mission statement to articulate the school's commitment and redirect existing policies and practices from tolerance for diversity to interactive pluralism.

Changes in institutional management can also influence retention. Clewell and Ficklen (1986) report key elements of successful retention efforts at four institutions: establishing institutional policies to enhance minority student retention; demonstrating an institutional commitment to minority student success; institutionalizing the program; establishing an institutional climate which is inclusive; providing comprehensive services through dedicated staff; collecting adequate data; developing faculty support for the program; and avoiding stigmatization of the participants. Barnhardt (1994) compiled a literature review that focuses on developing a strategy to improve the academic success of American Indian students. She found that model institutions have: mission statements that celebrate diversity; administrative involvement; linkages with minority communities; strong and numerous student support services; involvement of academic departments; active recruiting of minority faculty members; training and rewards for all faculty for developing multicultural approaches in teaching and research; and a multicultural emphasis for all students. Those in faculty and administrative positions play an important part in shaping the ethos of a campus, reiterating Bensimon's findings. Similarly, Santiago (1996) discusses the increased Latino/a student graduation rates associated with having a more diversified faculty and administration.

Richardson (1989, 1991) and Richardson and Skinner (1990a, 1990b) have explored mechanisms to develop a model of institutional change to improve the climate for diversity. In one study (1989), Richardson used case studies to analyze the effect of state policy, institutional mission, and organizational culture on the achievement of African American, Latino/a, and American Indian students. The universities were at one of three stages in improving equity outcomes: an emphasis on increasing student diversity carried out mostly by the student affairs staff; an attempt to cope with the high attrition rates and dissatisfaction produced in the first stage; and a fundamental shift in the organizational culture brought about with intensive faculty involvement. Moving institutions through these three stages requires strong leadership and action in strategic planning, coordination and control of implementation activities, articulation with community colleges, hiring and tenure procedures, faculty rewards and incentives, and student recruitment and cultural awareness.

In a further analysis of institutions, Richardson (1991) found that outcomes achieved by public institutions with exemplary records in minority student success had administrative commitment and strategic planning that demonstrated clearly that diversity and quality need not be pursued as mutually exclusive objectives. Institutional interventions throughout the university, in central administration, academic affairs, and student affairs, all play a part in the organizational culture that affects student diversity and achievement. Recent national evaluation studies have also linked curricular change, diversity in leadership, institutional commitment and intentionality, and community links to institutional effectiveness (Musil, García, Moses, and Smith 1995; Nettles and Hudgins 1995; Sedlacek 1995).

From this series of studies which examine student outcomes across a broad range of institutions, we may conclude that an institutional emphasis on creating a strong multicultural educational environment has positive effects on students' satisfaction with college, cultural awareness and commitment to promoting racial understanding after graduation. These findings hold regardless of a student's background or entering characteristics. When we consider also that supportive diversity programs have a positive effect on the persistence and achievement of students who might otherwise have fallen away, we can reasonably conclude that campus diversity efforts, in all their complex variety, do indeed work.

American higher education has just begun to focus on truly comprehensive efforts to create academic institutions that are committed to diversity and to educating students to comprehend, understand, and develop the intellectual and interpersonal capacities for living and working in complex and diverse American and global societies. Three critical findings stand out in the literature: 1) Where there are strong efforts to create an institutional climate that focuses on diversity as a significant aspect of living and learning in the educational institution, student satisfaction, cultural awareness, and commitment to racial understanding increase. These findings, however, also show that we have a long way to go before many groups feel welcomed and reflected in the intellectual and social culture of the campus; 2) Special purpose institutions have demonstrated powerful and positive effects on the self esteem, intellectual development, and after-college success of their students. This research should reassure us that a diversity of types of college

AN INSTITUTIONAL EMPHASIS ON CREATING A STRONG MULTICULTURAL EDUCATIONAL ENVIRONMENT HAS POSITIVE EFFECTS ON STUDENTS' SATISFACTION WITH COLLEGE, CULTURAL AWARENESS AND COMMITMENT TO PROMOTING RACIAL UNDERSTANDING AFTER GRADUATION.

campuses is necessary to national higher education goals. Yet the research on these campuses needs to be expanded to study how these institutions are addressing the education of their students to the full range of populations and perspectives represented across a diverse continuum of identities and interests; and 3) As these studies indicate, there is no substitute for moral, ethical, and intellectual academic leadership.

The Road Ahead

This report provides a multidimensional framework for analyzing diversity initiatives and the impact they have on college students. Using this framework, we have presented a developing and complex picture of the way different campus diversity strategies work together to provide productive educational support for students who, until very recently, have been underserved, silenced or almost entirely excluded from higher education.

Using this same framework, we have also observed that diversity efforts, from access to campus climate to curriculum change to comprehensive institutional transformation, provide demonstrable benefits to *all* students, whatever their backgrounds and characteristics. The students themselves are our most consistent source for this finding. It is they who report that diversity initiatives make a positive difference to their satisfaction with college; it is they who report that experiencing and studying diversity on campus makes a long-term difference to their cultural awareness and interest in fostering greater racial understanding and equity. Many studies also cite data from institutional records and faculty observations which serve to validate student reports.

CLEAR PATTERNS IN THE RESEARCH SHOW THE EDUCATIONAL AND SOCIAL VALUE OF DIVERSITY IN ITS MULTIPLE CAMPUS MEANINGS.

We observed at the outset of this analysis that change in the larger society is clearly driving much of higher education's focus on campus diversity. It is therefore very good news that higher education's efforts in this regard are demonstrably fostering intellectual development, cultural knowledge, equity interests and interracial understanding in college students. These outcomes are surely a resource in a society that is rapidly becoming intercultural, both at home and abroad.

As financial resources for higher education continue to be constrained and especially as opponents vigorously call for an end to identity-conscious corrective policies in higher education, it is important that policy-makers consider carefully the kinds of findings reviewed here. Nationally, there have been urgent cries that we know too little about the educational effects of diversity on campus. The failure to share what we actually know has left higher education silent in the face of those who wrongly contend that diversity on campus is lowering standards, deepening divisions, or is draining resources. Soberingly, it has left our campuses vulnerable to legally forced reversals of the very commitment to diversity in admissions which makes everything else reported in this study possible.

The reality is that there are clear patterns emerging in the research reviewed here. These patterns reveal the educational and social value of diversity in its multiple campus meanings. When doors open and previously excluded students find mentoring in educationally focused, challenging, supportive environments, they succeed in significant numbers. Their success belies the national fiction that only high test scores can predict positive educational outcomes.

Similarly, as the curriculum broadens to include voices and values previously excluded, students from all backgrounds clearly benefit from the experience. They develop knowledge, cultural interests and interracial understandings that seem to last well past graduation. The curriculum whose effects are reported here is more than the assigned reading for a course. The diversity curriculum also includes diversity in the classroom and on campus, the multiplicity of perspectives, the engagement with questions that are immediately real and significant to those who encounter them. These are important sources of social capital for a nation that, barely fifty years hence, will no longer be majority white.

Diversity initiatives and diversity research are often "segregated" as though they hold significance only for designated populations. In truth, the research reported here has the most powerful implications for campuses as a whole. Higher education is rightly subject to criticism that far too many of those who enter its doors fall away. Retention rates and graduation rates are much too low. This is an issue that cuts across all populations. It is not particular to selected groups, even though it has been most carefully studied in the context of designated populations.

THE RESEARCH REPORTED HERE HAS THE MOST POWERFUL IMPLICATIONS FOR CAMPUSES AS A WHOLE.

The research reported here illuminates a range of educational strategies that can effectively raise our levels of success, not just with specific students but with all students. The successful campus diversity strategies reported in these pages are commonly used, not just in multicultural offices and programs but also in nationally known institutions distinguished by their high graduation rates and high levels of student attainment.

These strategies which the research clearly suggests are "working" can be incorporated at every campus. High expectations, mentoring, targeted challenge and support, productive involvement with peers and faculty, programs tailored to students' known educational needs and risks, a supportive classroom and educational environment, direct engagement with challenging and significant social issues—these strategies which work for "diverse students" also work powerfully for any students. But activities which "work" seem to work best in institutions where campus climate has been addressed, where the imperative of diversity is seen as central to the mission, and where the academic, educational, and intellectual reasons for engaging diversity in the society are clearly understood.

Moreover, the research results support the need to develop understandings of diversity which do not pit the initiatives that are important to one dimension of diversity against those that are appropriate for other dimensions. Indeed, more often than not, approaches which support and sustain individual groups coexist comfortably with or enhance strategies in other domains.

Even as we observe the significance of many success stories, it important that we face the limitations of our current knowledge. Much more work is needed, both qualitative and quantitative, to identify the unique experiences and issues faced by Asian Americans, American Indians, women of all colors, first generation college students, gays, lesbians, bisexuals, and disabled students. In addition, more research is needed to show the effects of diversity initiatives, not only on students of color, but on white students as well.

Above all higher education needs research that carefully probes the complexities of diversity issues and strategies. It is already clear, for example, that the identity categories which have guided much of this research are not only complex but undergoing significant reconfiguration. We need to know much more than we do about students who claim membership in multiple categories. They are not only the faces of tomorrow but a present reality at all institutions.

We also need comparative studies. The most promising research reported here illuminates the success of institutions that have taken diversity seriously, at all levels and in all parts of the campus. But many campuses, we know, have not done this. At many institutions, diversity is still assigned to a single office, often laboring uphill against the combined forces of inertia, resistance and competing priorities. At such campuses, diversity programs frequently fail for lack of support. We need more studies that show empirically not only what works, but also what does not.

As research on campus diversity moves forward, studies need to be multivariate and longitudinal, examining results within and across institutions. Snapshots at a point in time are not as beneficial as those studies showing changes from interventions over time. Research needs to be open-minded, relevant to policy discussions, and attentive to the cost/benefit outcomes of diversity investments.

DIVERSITY ON CAMPUS IMPELS US TO PREPARE STUDENTS AND OUR INSTITUTIONS FOR A FUTURE IN WHICH THE DIVERSITY OF OUR COMMUNITIES AND INSTITUTIONS IS WIDELY RECOGNIZED AS A POWERFUL RESOURCE.

Institutions need to build evaluation components into their programs to determine whether or not, based on given criteria, a diversity program is successful and whether the program has validity for a given population. There are resources available to assist in this effort (e.g. Sedlacek, 1994; Smith, Wolf and Levitan, 1994). The appropriateness of a program needs to be addressed, its institutional context explored, and the level of institutionalization of the program evaluated, so that results, positive and negative, can contribute to the national discussion about effectiveness in serving the extraordinarily diverse students who now flock to our campuses.

There is no one-shot program or solution for diversity. Diversity in higher education should not even be viewed as a problem that is in need of a solution. Indeed, it is apparent that engaging diversity provides a wonderful opportunity to attend to many issues which have long needed attention—teaching and learning, curricular coherence, assessment, campus-community connections, climate, student success, and advising, among others. Diversity on campus impels us to prepare students and our institutions for a future in which the diversity of our communities and institutions is widely recognized as a powerful resource. As we see from this report, many colleges and universities in American higher education are already seizing this opportunity.

The study of diversity on campus is an evolving, multi-dimensional field. Many different groups and issues fall under the umbrella of diversity, each with its own unique history and context within higher education and each intersecting across multiple and simultaneous differences. But diversity is finally not about the needs of one or another group competing for scarce resources. It is rather about purposeful and effective designs for supporting all students' educational achievement. As such, it is an integral component of the mission and purpose of the institution, and essential to whether our institutions are or will be positioned to educate all students for full participation in the economic, social, and civic domains of a diverse society.

References

Abdullahi, I. 1992. Recruitment and mentoring of minority students. *Journal of Library and Information Science* 33 (4): 307–310.

Adams, M. C., and E. Wadsworth, eds. 1989. *The role of the faculty in meeting the national need for African American, American Indian, and Latino scholars.* Stony Brook, NY: State University of New York. ERIC, ED 327598.

Adams, M., and Y. Zhou-McGovern. 1994. The sociomoral development of undergraduates in a "social diversity" course: Developmental theory, research, and instructional applications. Paper presented at the annual meeting of the American Educational Research Association, April, at New Orleans, LA.

Adelman, C. 1997. Diversity: Walk the walk, and drop the talk. *Change* 29 (4): 35–45.

Allen, W. R. 1992. The color of success: African-American college student outcomes at predominantly White and historically Black public colleges and universities. *Harvard Educational Review* 62 (1): 26–44.

Andrew, L. D., and R. Russo. 1989. Who gets what?: Impact of financial aid policies. *Research in Higher Education* 30:471–483.

Antony, J. 1993. Can we all get along?: How college impacts students' sense of the importance of promoting racial understanding. Paper presented at the annual meeting of the Association for the Study of Higher Education, November, at Pittsburgh, PA. ERIC, ED 365174.

Appel, M., D. Cartwright, D. G. Smith, and L. E. Wolf. 1996. *The impact of diversity on students: A preliminary review of the research literature.* Washington, DC: Association of American Colleges and Universities.

Asera, R., and P. U. Treisman. 1995. Routes to mathematics for African American, Latino and Native American students in the 1990s: The educational trajectories of summer mathematics institute participants. In *Changing the culture: Mathematics education in the research community,* edited by N. D. Fisher, H. B. Keynes, and P. D. Wagreich. CBMS Issues in Mathematics Education, vol. 5. American Mathematical Society.

Association of American Colleges. 1995. *The drama of diversity and democracy: Higher education and American Commitments.* Washington, DC: AAC&U.

Astin, A. W. 1984. Student involvement: A developmental theory for higher education. *Journal of College Student Development* 25:297-308.

——. 1991. *Assessment for excellence: The philosophy and practice of assessment and evaluation in higher education.* New York: American Council on Education/Macmillan.

——. 1993. *What matters in college?: Four critical years revisited.* San Francisco: Jossey-Bass.

Banta, T. W., ed. 1993. *Making a difference: Outcomes of a decade of assessment in higher education.* San Francisco: Jossey-Bass.

Bargad, A., and J. S. Hyde. 1991. Women's studies: A study of feminist identity development in women. *Psychology of Women Quarterly* 15:181-201.

Barnhardt, C. 1994. Life on the other side: Native student survival in a university world. *Peabody Journal of Education* 69 (2): 115-139.

Beckham-Chasnoff, S. 1996. Homophobic attitude change. Ph.D. dissertation, Indiana State University, Terre Haute. Abstract in *Dissertation Abstracts International* 57 (09): 5974B.

Belgarde, W. L. 1992. The history of American Indian community colleges. In *ASHE reader series: Racial and ethnic diversity in higher education*, edited by C. Turner, M. Garcia, A. Nora, and L. I. Rendón. Needham Heights, MA: Simon and Schuster.

Bell, E. D., and R. W. Drakeford. 1992. A case study of the Black student peer mentor program at the University of North Carolina–Greensboro in Fall 1987. *College Student Journal* 26:381-386.

Bennett, C., and A. M. Okinaka. 1990. Factors related to persistence among Asian, Black, Hispanic, and White undergraduates at a predominantly White university: Comparison between first and fourth year cohorts. *Urban Review* 22 (1): 33-60.

Benns-Suter, R. 1993. *The utilization of simulations in multicultural education.* Millersville, PA: Millersville University. ERIC, ED 364613.

Bensimon, E. 1995. *Creating an institutional identity out of differences: A case study of multicultural organizational change.* University Park: Pennsylvania State University.

Bidell, T. R., E. M. Lee, N. Bouchie, C. Ward, and D. Brass. 1994. Developing conceptions of racism among young White adults in the context of cultural diversity coursework. Paper presented at the annual meeting of the American Educational Research Association, April, at New Orleans, LA. ERIC, ED 377270.

Bonsangue, M. V., and D. E. Drew. 1995. Increasing minority students' success in calculus. In *Fostering student success in quantitative gateway courses*, edited by J. Gainen and E. W. Willemsen. New Directions for Teaching and Learning, no. 61. San Francisco: Jossey-Bass.

Boyer, P. 1997. *Native American colleges: Progress and prospects.* Princeton, NJ: Carnegie Foundation for the Advancement of Teaching.

California Postsecondary Education Commission. 1992. *Resource guide for assessing campus climate.* Sacramento, CA.

Capoor, M., and D. Overstreet. 1993. Assessment of multiple treatments used to help underprepared students. Paper presented at the annual meeting of the Association for Institutional Research, May, at Chicago, IL.

Carnegie Foundation for the Advancement of Teaching. 1989. *Tribal colleges: Shaping the future of Native America. A special report.* Lawrenceville, NJ: Princeton University Press.

Carter, D. J., and R. Wilson. 1997. *Minorities in Higher Education.* Washington, DC: American Council on Education.

Chan, K. S., and L. C. Wang. 1991. Racism and the model minority: Asian Americans in higher education. In *The racial crisis in American higher education*, edited by P. G. Altbach and K. Lomotey. New York: State University of New York Press.

Chang, M. J. 1996. Racial diversity in higher education: Does a racially mixed student population affect educational outcomes? Ph.D. dissertation, University of California, Los Angeles. Abstract in *Dissertation Abstracts International* 57 (04): 1513A.

Chen, S. 1995. On the ethnic studies requirement. In *The Asian American educational experience*, edited by D. T. Nakanishi and T. Y. Nishida. New York: Routledge.

Chesler, M. A., and X. Zúñiga. 1991. Dealing with prejudice and conflict in the classroom: The pink triangle exercise. *Teaching Sociology* 19:173-181.

Childers, M. 1997. -Ism (n.): Lessons learned from the National Video Diversity Project. *Change* 29 (2): 33-37.

Clewell, B. C., and M. S. Ficklen. 1986. *Improving minority retention in higher education: A search for effective institutional practices.* Princeton, NJ: Educational Testing Service. ERIC, ED 299841.

Conciatore, J. 1990. From flunking to mastering calculus: Treisman's retention model proves to be "too good" on some campuses. *Black Issues in Higher Education* 6 (22): 5-6.

Corley, T. J., and R. H. Pollack. 1996. Do changes in the stereotypic depiction of a lesbian couple affect heterosexuals' attitudes toward lesbianism? *Journal of Homosexuality* 32 (2): 1-17.

Cross, K. P. 1974. *Beyond the open door: New students in higher education.* San Francisco: Jossey-Bass.

Croteau, J. M., and M. T. Kusek. 1992. Gay and lesbian speaker panels: Implementation and research. *Journal of Counseling and Development* 70:396-401.

Curtis, D. E., and J. Heritage. 1991. Influencing homonegative attitudes in college students through an educational unit on homosexuality. Paper presented at the meeting of the Middle Tennessee Psychological Association, April, at Nashville, TN. ERIC, ED 346388.

D'Augelli, A. R. 1992. Lesbian and gay male undergraduates' experiences of harassment and fear on campus. *Journal of Interpersonal Violence* 7:383-395.

D'Augelli, A. R., and S. L. Hershberger. 1993. African American undergraduates on a predominantly White campus: Academic factors, social networks, and campus climate. *Journal of Negro Education* 62 (1): 67-79.

Davis, J. 1994. College in Black and White: Campus environment and academic achievement of African American males. *Journal of Negro Education* 63:620-633.

Duster, T. 1995. They're taking over! and other myths about race on campus. In *Higher education under fire: Politics, economics, and the crisis of the humanities*, edited by M. Bérubé and C. Nelson. New York: Routledge.

Education Commission of the States. 1990. *Minority achievement counting on you. Responding to student diversity: A community college perspective.* Denver, CO.

Faison, J. 1993. Unmeasured but essential: Distinguishing factors between African American graduate school persisters and non-persisters. Ph.D. dissertation, Emory University.

———. 1996. The next generation: The mentoring of African American graduate students on predominantly White university campuses. Paper presented at the annual meeting of the American Education Research Association, New York.

Falk, D., and L. P. Aitken. 1984. Promoting retention among American Indian college students. *Journal of American Indian Education* 23 (2): 24-31.

Fischer, B., and D. Hartmann. 1995. The impact of race on the social experience of college students at a predominantly White university. *Journal of Black Studies* 26 (2): 117-133.

Fleming, J. 1985. *Blacks in college: A comparative study of students' success in black and white institutions.* San Francisco: Jossey-Bass. ERIC, ED 266745.

Francis, P. L. 1993. Assessing the effectiveness of multicultural curriculum initiatives in higher education: Proving the self-evident. In *Strategies for implementation in colleges and universities*, edited by J. Q. Adams and J. R. Welsch. Multicultural Education, vol. 3. Macomb, IL: Western Illinois University.

Fuertes, J. N., M. Cothran, and W. E. Sedlacek. 1991. A model for increasing Hispanic student involvement on U.S. campuses. *College Student Affairs Journal* 11 (2): 11-15.

Fuertes, J. N., and W. E. Sedlacek. 1995. Using noncognitive variables to predict the grades and retention of Hispanic students. *College Student Affairs Journal* 14 (2): 30-36.

Fullilove, R. E., and P. U. Treisman. 1990. Mathematics achievement among African American undergraduates at the University of California, Berkeley: An evaluation of the mathematics workshop program. *Journal of Negro Education* 59:463-478.

Garmon, M. A. 1996. Missed messages: How prospective teachers' racial attitudes mediate what they learn from a course on diversity. Ph.D. dissertation, Michigan State University. Abstract in *Dissertation Abstracts International* 57 (09): 3896A.

Geasler, M. J., J. M. Croteau, C. J. Heineman, and C. J. Edlund. 1995. A qualitative study of students' expression of change after attending panel presentations by lesbian, gay, and bisexual speakers. *Journal of College Student Development* 36:483-492.

Gilbert, W. S. 1996. Bridging the gap between high school and college: A successful program that promotes academic success for Hopi and Navajo students. Paper presented at the Retention in Education for Today's American Indian Nations conference, April, at Tucson, AZ. ERIC, ED 398039.

Gilliard, M. D. 1996. Racial climate and institutional support factors affecting success in predominantly White institutions: An examination of African-American and White student experiences. Ph.D. dissertation, University of Michigan. Abstract in *Dissertation Abstracts International* 57 (04): 1515A.

Gobbo, K., and J. A. Bolaski. 1997. Understanding the concerns of college students with learning disabilities and attention deficit disorders. *Student Affairs Journal–Online* [online]. Available at http://www.sajo.org.

Grant, C. A., and W. G. Secada. 1990. Preparing teachers for diversity. In *Handbook of research in teacher education*, edited by W. R. Houston. New York: Macmillan. ERIC, ED 318735.

Green, S., P. Dixon, and V. Gold-Neil. 1993. The effects of a gay/lesbian panel discussion on college student attitudes toward gay men, lesbians, and persons with AIDS (PWAs). *Journal of Sex Education and Therapy* 19 (1): 47-63.

Guarasci, R. 1997. Community-based learning and intercultural citizenship. In *Democratic education in an age of difference: Redefining citizenship in higher education*, edited by R. Guarasci and G. H. Cornwell. San Francisco: Jossey-Bass.

Guarasci, R., and G. H. Cornwell, eds. 1997. *Democratic education in an age of difference Redefining citizenship in higher education*. San Francisco: Jossey-Bass.

Guon, D. G. 1988. Minority access and retention: An evaluation of a multi-university peer counseling program. Paper presented at a meeting of the Midwestern Psychological Association, at Chicago, IL.

Harwarth, I., M. Maline, and E. DeBra. 1997. *Women's colleges in the United States: History, issues, and challenges*. Washington, DC: National Institute on Postsecondary Education, Libraries, and Lifelong Learning, U.S. Department of Education.

Hasslen, R. C. 1993. The effects of teaching strategies in multicultural education on monocultural students' perceptions. Ph.D. dissertation, University of Minnesota. Abstract in *Dissertation Abstracts International* 55 (01): 4668A.

Herek, G. M. 1993. Documenting prejudice against lesbians and gay men on campus: The Yale sexual orientation survey. *Journal of Homosexuality* 25 (4): 15-31.

Hummel, M. L. 1997. Eliminating the achievement gap: The 21st Century Program. *About Campus* 1 (6): 28-29.

Hummel, M. L., and C. Steele. 1996. The learning community: A program to address issues of academic achievement and retention. *Journal of Intergroup Relations* 23 (2): 28-33.

Humphreys, D., and C. Schneider. 1997. Curricular change gains momentum: New requirements focus on diversity and social responsibility. *Diversity Digest* 1 (2): 1-5.

Hune, S. 1997. Higher education as gendered space: Asian-American women and everyday inequities. In *Everyday sexism in the third millennium,* edited by C. Rambo Ronai, B. A. Zsembik, and J. R. Feagin. New York: Routledge.

Hune, S., and K. S. Chan. 1997. *Special focus: Asian Pacific American demographic and educational trends. Fifteenth annual status report.* Washington, DC: American Council on Education.

Hurtado, S., and D. F. Carter. 1994. Latino students' sense of belonging in the college community: Rethinking the concept of integration on campus. Paper presented at the annual meeting of the American Educational Research Association, April, at New Orleans, LA.

Hurtado, S., D. F. Carter, and A. Spuler. 1996. Latino student transition to college: Assessing difficulties and factors in successful college adjustment. *Research in Higher Education* 37:135-157.

Hurtado, S., E. L. Dey, and J. G. Treviño. 1994. Exclusion or self-segregation?: Interaction across racial/ethnic groups on college campuses. Paper presented at the annual meeting of the American Educational Research Association, April, at New Orleans, LA.

Hurtado, S., J. F. Milem, W. R. Allen, and A. R. Clayton-Pedersen. 1996. *Improving the climate for racial/ethnic diversity in higher education.* Report to the Common Destiny Alliance, College Park, MD.

Hyun, M. 1996. Commitment to change: How college impacts changes in students' commitment to racial understanding. Ph.D. dissertation, University of California, Los Angeles. Abstract in *Dissertation Abstracts International* 57 (05): 1978A.

Institute for the Study of Social Change. 1995. Reprint. *The Diversity Project: Final report.* Berkeley, CA: University of California. Original edition, 1991.

Johnson, A. W., and J. A. Sullivan. 1995. Mentoring program practices and effectiveness. In *Mentoring: New strategies and challenges,* edited by M. W. Galbraith and N. H. Cohen. New Directions for Adult and Continuing Education, no. 66. San Francisco: Jossey-Bass.

Kardia, D. B. 1996. Diversity's closet: Student attitudes toward lesbians, gay men, and bisexual people on a multicultural campus. Ph.D. dissertation, University of Michigan. Abstract in *Dissertation Abstracts International* 57 (03): 1090A.

Kayabasi, M. 1988. Does the City College New World Civilization course reduce provincialism? Paper presented at the annual meeting of the Northeastern Educational Research Association, May. ERIC, ED 350207.

Keim, J., J. McWhirter, and B. Berstein. 1996. Academic success and university accommodation for learning disabilities: Is there a relationship? *Journal of College Student Development* 37:502-509.

Kibble, J. F., M. A. Malmberg, and S. H. Ratwik. 1990. Capturing the experience of Native American persisters: The exit interview vehicle. Paper presented at the annual meeting of the American Educational Research Association, April, at Boston, MA.

Lang, M., and C. A. Ford. 1992. *Strategies for retaining minority students in higher education.* Springfield, IL: Charles C. Thomas.

LaSalle, L. A., and R. A. Rhoads. 1992. Exploring campus intolerance: A textual analysis of comments concerning lesbian, gay and bisexual people. Paper presented at the annual meeting of the American Educational Research Association, April, at San Francisco. ERIC, ED 349497.

LeSure, G. E. 1993. Ethnic differences and the effects of racism on college adjustment. Paper presented at the annual meeting of the American Psychological Association, August, at Toronto, Canada. ERIC, ED 367936.

Livingston, M., and R. Steward. 1987. Minority students on a White campus: Perception is truth. *NASPA Journal* 24:39-49.

Lomotey, K. 1990a. Culture and its artifacts in higher education: Their impact on the enrollment and retention of African-American students. Paper presented at the annual meeting of the American Educational Research Association, April, at Boston, MA. ERIC, ED 319332.

——. 1990b. The retention of African-American students: The effects of institutional arrangements in higher education. Paper presented at the annual meeting of the American Educational Research Association, April, at Boston, MA. ERIC, ED 319333.

Lopez, G. E. 1993. The effect of group contact and curriculum on White, Asian American, and African American students' attitudes. Ph.D. dissertation, University of Michigan. Abstract in *Dissertation Abstracts International* 54 (07): 3900B.

Luebke, B. F., and M. E. Reilly. 1995. *Women's studies graduates: The first generation.* New York: Teachers College Press. ERIC, ED 390312.

Maher, F. A., and M. K. T. Tetrault. 1994. *The feminist classroom.* New York: Basic Books.

Maluso, D. 1992. Interventions to lessen racist prejudice and discrimination among college students. Ph.D. dissertation, University of Rhode Island. Abstract in *Dissertation Abstracts International* 53 (08): 4423B.

Marchesani, J. J. 1994. Constellation prizes: Using science fiction for lesbian, gay, and bisexual issues in college classes. Paper presented at the Conference on College Composition and Communication, March, at Nashville, TN. ERIC, ED 370117.

McGrath, P., and F. Galaviz. 1996. The Puente Project. *About Campus* 1 (5): 27-28, 30.

Minner, S., V. Bizardi, V. Arthur, J. Chischille, J. Holiday, R. Pyron, A. Rezzonico, and B. Yellowhair. 1995. Completing university degrees: Barriers for Native Americans. Paper presented at the meeting of the American Council on Rural Special Education, March, at Las Vegas, NV. ERIC, ED 381302.

Moore, T. L., and C. Reeves-Kazelskis. 1992. Effects of formal instruction on preservice teachers' beliefs about multicultural education. Paper presented at the annual meeting of the Mid-South Educational Research Association, November, at Knoxville, TN. ERIC, ED 354231.

Mow, S. L., and M. T. Nettles. 1993. Minority student access to, and persistence and performance in, college: A review of the trends and research literature. In *Higher education: Handbook of theory and research,* edited by J. C. Smart. New York: Agathon Press.

Musil, C. M., ed. 1992. *The courage to question: Women's studies and student learning.* Washington, DC: Association of American Colleges. ERIC, ED 347890.

Musil, C. M., M. García, Y. Moses, and D. Smith. 1995. *Diversity in higher education: A work in progress.* Washington, DC: Association of American Colleges and Universities.

Myers, S. L. 1997. Why diversity is a smoke screen for affirmative action. *Change* 29 (4): 24-32.

Nagasawa, R., and D. J. Espinosa. 1992. Educational achievement and the adaptive strategy of Asian American college students: Facts, theory, and hypotheses. *Journal of College Student Development* 33:137-142.

Nelson, E. S., and S. L. Krieger. 1997. Changes in attitudes toward homosexuality in college students: Implementation of a gay men and lesbian peer panel. *Journal of Homosexuality* 33 (2): 63-81.

Nelson, N. J., C. Johnson, J. Boyd, and T. Scott. 1994. The effects of participation in an intergroup communication program: An assessment of Shippensburg University's Building Bridges program. Paper presented at the annual meeting of the Eastern Psychological Association, April, at Providence, RI. ERIC, ED 370152.

Nelson, W. 1994. Receptivity to institutional assistance: An important variable for African American and Mexican American student achievement. *Journal of College Student Development* 35:378-384.

Nesbitt, L., Jr., et al. 1994. On racial sensitivity training for college freshmen: A survey of institutional opinions and practices. *Journal of Blacks in Higher Education* (3): 77-79.

Nettles, M. T. 1990a. Success in doctoral programs: Experiences of minority and White students. *American Journal of Education* 98:494-521.

——, ed. 1990b. *The effect of assessment on minority student participation.* New Directions for Institutional Research, no. 65. San Francisco: Jossey-Bass.

Nettles, M. T., and C. Hudgins. 1995. *An evaluation of Philip Morris Companies, Inc. Tolerance on campus: Establishing common ground.* Colby College and Northern Illinois University.

Nora, A. 1987. Determinants of retention among Chicano college students: A structural model. *Research in Higher Education* 26:31-59.

——. 1990. Campus-based aid programs as determinants of retention among Hispanic community college students. *Journal of Higher Education* 61:312-331.

Nora, A., A. Hagedorn, A. Cabrera, and E. T. Pascarella. 1994. Differential impacts of academic and social experiences on college-related behavioral outcomes across different ethnic and gender groups at four-year institutions. Paper presented at the annual meeting of the American Educational Research Association, April, at New Orleans, LA.

Nottingham, C. R., D. H. Rosen, and C. Parks. 1992. Psychological well-being among African American university students. *Journal of College Student Development* 33:356-362.

Ortíz, A. M. 1995. Promoting racial understanding in college students: A study of educational and developmental interventions. Paper presented at the annual meeting of the Association for the Study of Higher Education, November, at Orlando, FL.

Osajima, K. 1995. Racial politics and the invisibility of Asian Americans in higher education. *Educational Foundations* 9 (1): 35-53.

Pascarella, E. T., and P. T. Terenzini. 1991. *How college affects students.* San Francisco: Jossey Bass.

Pascarella, E. T., M. I. Edison, A. Nora, L. S. Hagedorn, and P. T. Terenzini. 1996. Influences on students' openness to diversity and challenge in the first year of college. *Journal of Higher Education* 67:174-195.

Pascarella, E. T., E. J. Whitt, A. Nora, M. Edison, L. S. Hagedorn, and P. T. Terenzini. 1996. What have we learned from the first year of the National Study of Student Learning? *Journal of College Student Development* 37:182-192.

Pence, D. 1992. A women's studies course: Its impact on women's attitudes toward men and masculinity. *National Women's Studies Association Journal* 4:321-335.

Pettigrew, T. F. 1994. Prejudice and discrimination on the college campus. *The HEES Review* 6 (1) [online]. Available at http://www.review.org/issues/vol6no1.html.

Piskur, J., and D. Degelman. 1992. Effect of reading a summary of research about biological bases of homosexual orientation on attitudes toward homosexuals. *Psychological Reports* 7:219-1225.

Powers, S. M. 1996. An implementation study of hypermedia-based multicultural training. Ed.D. dissertation, University of Virginia. Abstract in *Dissertation Abstracts International* 57 (08): 3467A.

Richardson, R. C., Jr. 1989. Changing organizational culture to accommodate student diversity. Paper presented at a meeting of the Society for College and University Planning, at Denver, CO.

——. 1991. *Promoting fair college outcomes: Learning from the experiences of the past decade.* Denver, CO: Education Commission of the States. ERIC, ED 329179.

Richardson, R. C., Jr., and E. F. Skinner. 1990a. *Achieving quality and diversity: Universities in a multicultural society.* New York: Macmillan. ERIC, ED 327093.

——. 1990b. Adapting to diversity: Organizational influences on student achievement. *Journal of Higher Education* 61: 485-511.

Riordan, C. 1992. Single- and mixed-gender colleges for women: Educational, attitudinal, and occupational outcomes. *Review of Higher Education* 15:327-346.

Runyan, M. K. 1991. The effect of extra time on reading comprehension scores for university students with and without learning disabilities. *Journal of Learning Disabilities* 24 (2): 104-108.

St. John, E. P. 1991. The impact of student financial aid: A review of recent research. *Journal of Student Financial Aid* 21 (1): 18-32.

Santiago, I. S. 1996. Increasing the Latino leadership pipeline: Institutional and organizational strategies. In *Achieving administrative diversity*, edited by I. H. Johnson and A. J. Ottens. New Directions for Student Services, no. 74. San Francisco: Jossey-Bass.

Schoem, D. 1996. Intergroup relations, conflict, and community. In *Democratic education in an age of difference: Redefining citizenship in higher education*, edited by R. Guarasci and G. H. Cornwell. San Francisco: Jossey-Bass.

Sedlacek, W. E. 1994. Issues in advancing diversity through assessment. *Journal of Counseling and Development* 72:549-553.

——. 1995. *Improving racial and ethnic diversity and campus climate at four-year independent Midwest colleges: An evaluation report of the Lilly Endowment Grant Program.* College Park: University of Maryland.

Sharma, M. P., and J. S. Mulka. 1993. The impact of international education upon United States students in comparative perspective. Paper presented at the annual meeting of the Comparative and International Education Society, March, at Kingston, Jamaica. ERIC, ED 358800.

Smith, D. G. 1990. Women's colleges and coed colleges: Is there a difference for women? *Journal of Higher Education* 61:181-197.

———. 1995. Organizational implications of diversity in higher education. In *Diversity in organizations: New perspectives for a changing workplace*, edited by M. M. Chemers, S. Oskamp, and M. A. Costanzo. Thousand Oaks, CA: Sage.

———. 1997. How diversity influences learning. *Liberal Education* 83 (2): 42-47.

Smith, D. G., L. E. Wolf, and T. Levitan, eds. 1994. *Studying diversity in higher education*. New Directions for Institutional Research, no. 81. San Francisco: Jossey-Bass.

Smith, D. G., L. E. Wolf, and D. E. Morrison. 1995. Paths to success: Factors related to the impact of women's colleges. *Journal of Higher Education* 66:245-266.

Smith, K. M. 1992. Gender differences and the impact of college on White students' racial attitudes. Ph.D. dissertation, University of Michigan, Ann Arbor.

Solorzano, D. G. 1995. The doctorate production and baccalaureate origins of African Americans in the sciences and engineering. *Journal of Negro Education* 64:15-32.

Sparks, W. G., and M. E. Verner. 1993. *Intervention strategies in multicultural education: A comparison of pre-service models*. Normal: Illinois State University. ERIC, ED 354234.

Spitzburg, I. J., and V. V. Thorndike. 1992. *Creating community on college campuses*. Albany: State University of New York Press.

Springer, L., B. Palmer, P. T. Terenzini, E. T. Pascarella, and A. Nora. 1996. Attitudes toward campus diversity: Participation in a racial or cultural awareness workshop. *Review of Higher Education* 20:53-68.

Stake, J. E., and M. A. Gerner. 1987. The women's studies experience: Personal and professional gains for women and men. *Psychology of Women Quarterly* 11:277-284.

Steele, C. M. 1995. *Twenty-first Century Program and stereotype vulnerability*. Palo Alto, CA: Stanford University.

———. 1997. A threat in the air: How stereotypes shape intellectual identity and performance. *American Psychologist* 52:613-629.

Steele, C. M., and J. Aronson. 1995. Stereotype threat and the intellectual test performance of African Americans. *Journal of Personality and Social Psychology* 69:797-811.

Tafalla, R. J., R. Rivera, and B. Tuchel. 1993. Psychological factors related to minority persistence on a predominantly White campus. Paper presented at Minority Students Today: Recruitment, Retention, and Success, October, at San Antonio, TX.

Tanaka, G. K. 1996. The impact of multiculturalism on White students. Ph.D. dissertation, University of California, Los Angeles. Abstract in *Dissertation Abstracts International* 57 (05): 1980A.

Tate, D. S., and C. L. Schwartz. 1993. Increasing the retention of American Indian students in professional programs in higher education. *Journal of American Indian Education* 33 (1): 21-31.

Terrell, M., and S. Hassell. 1994. Mentoring undergraduate minority students: An overview, survey, and model program. In *Minorities in education*, edited by M. A. Wunsch. New Directions for Teaching and Learning, no. 57. San Francisco: Jossey-Bass.

Tidball, E. 1980. Women's colleges and women's achievers revisited. *Signs* 5:504-517.

Tierney, W. G. 1993. *Building communities of difference: Higher education in the twenty-first century*. Westport, CT: Bergin and Garvey.

——, ed. 1990. *Assessing academic climates and cultures*. New Directions for Institutional Research, no. 68. San Francisco: Jossey-Bass.

Tinto, V. 1993. *Leaving college: Rethinking the causes and cures of student attrition*. second edition. Chicago: University of Chicago Press.

Tinto, V. 1987. *Leaving college: Rethinking the causes and cures of student attrition*. Chicago: University of Chicago Press.

Treisman, P. U. 1988. A study of the mathematics performance of Black students at the University of California, Berkeley. In *Changing the culture: Mathematics education in the research community*, edited by N. D. Fisher, H. B. Keynes, and P. D. Wagreich. CBMS Issues in Mathematics Education, vol. 5. American Mathematical Society.

Trigg, M. K., and B. J. Balliet. 1997. Finding community across boundaries: Service learning in women's studies. In *Democratic education in an age of difference: Redefining citizenship in higher education*, edited by R. Guarasci and G. H. Cornwell. San Francisco: Jossey-Bass.

Trippi, J., and H. E. Cheatham. 1989. Effects of special counseling programs for Black freshmen on a predominantly White campus. *Journal of College Student Development* 30:35-40.

Turner, C. S. V. 1994. Guests in someone else's house: Students of color. *Review of Higher Education* 17:355-370.

University of Wisconsin, Stevens Point. 1992. *Which one of your ten friends is homosexual?: Understanding, accepting, and supporting*. National Association of College and University Residence Halls Report, no. N25D-92-005-12. Stevens Point: University of Wisconsin, Stevens Point [online]. Available at http://www.nacurh.okstate.edu/rfi/rfi_frame.html.

Varlotta, L. 1997. Invoking a university's mission statement to promote diversity, civility, and free speech. *NASPA Journal* 34:123-133.

Villalpando, O. 1994. Comparing the effects of multiculturalism and diversity on minority and White students' satisfaction with college. Paper presented at the annual meeting of the Association for the Study of Higher Education, November, at Tucson, AZ. ERIC, ED 375721.

Vogel, S. A., and P. B. Adelman. 1992. The success of college students with learning disabilities: Factors related to educational attainment. *Journal of Learning Disabilities* 25:430-441.

Walters, A. S. 1994. Using visual media to reduce homophobia: A classroom demonstration. *Journal of Sex Education and Therapy* 20 (2): 92-100.

Walters, A. S., and C. P. Phillips. 1994. Hurdles: An activity for homosexuality education. *Journal of Sex Education and Therapy* 20 (3): 198-203.

Watanabe, G. C. 1992. A comprehensive developmentally-based undergraduate diversity education model at Washington State University. Ed.D. dissertation, Washington State University. Abstract in *Dissertation Abstracts International* 53 (11): 3825A.

Watson, L., and G. Kuh. 1996. The influences of dominant race environments on student involvement, perceptions, and educational gains: A look at historically Black and predominantly White liberal arts institutions. *Journal of College Student Development* 37:415-420.

Wenzlaff, T. L., and A. Biewer. 1996. Research: Native American students define factors for success. *Tribal College* 7 (4): 40-44.

Wilson, K. B. 1994. Developing a freshman mentoring program: A small college experience. In *Minorities in education*, edited by M. A. Wunsch. New Directions for Teaching and Learning, no. 57. San Francisco: Jossey-Bass.

Wolf, L. E. 1995. Models of excellence: The baccalaureate origins of successful European American women, African American women, and Latinas. Ph.D. dissertation, Claremont Graduate School, CA.

Wright, B. 1990. American Indian studies programs: Surviving the '80s, thriving in the '90s. *Journal of American Indian Education* 30 (1): 17-24.

Wright, B., and P. W. Head. 1990. Tribally controlled community colleges: A student outcomes assessment of associate degree recipients. *Community College Review* 18 (3): 28-33.

Zúñiga, X., B. A. Nagda, T. D. Sevig, M. Thompson, and E. L. Dey. 1995. Speaking the unspeakable: Student learning outcomes in intergroup dialogues on a college campus. Paper presented at the annual meeting of the Association for the Study of Higher Education, November, at Orlando, FL.

Zúñiga, X., C. M. Vasques, T. D. Sevig, and B. A. Nagda. n.d. *Dismantling walls and building bridges: Student experiences in inter-race/inter-ethnic dialogues.* Available from the Program on Intergroup Relations, Conflict and Community, 3000 Michigan Union, 530 South State Street, Ann Arbor, MI 48105-1349.

Annotated Bibliography

Aaronsohn, E., M. Howell, and C. J. Carter. 1993. Preparing monocultural teachers for a multicultural world: Attitudes toward inner-city schools. *Equity and excellence in education* 28 (1): 5–9.

This study was designed to determine the effect that exposure to inner city schools had on college students' unexamined assumptions about inner city children in terms of race and social class. Subjects in this study were first-generation whites enrolled in selected graduate and undergraduate classes in a teacher education program. Faculty members used a variety of methods to expose students to the realities of inner city schools. Subjects were asked to "free-write" their impressions of inner city schools and inner city students at the beginning and end of the semester. The results indicate significant shifts over time in self-reported perspectives toward more complexity and openness with respect to the inner city. In other words, the intervention was judged to have had a positive effect on the teacher education students.

Adams, M., and Y. Zhou-McGovern. 1994. The sociomoral development of under-graduates in a "social diversity" course: Developmental theory, research, and instructional applications. Paper presented at the annual meeting of the American Educational Research Association, April, at New Orleans, LA.

This paper considers whether theories of cognitive development can shed light upon the processes of social justice and social diversity education. It presents evidence of cognitive developmental change in a college-level social diversity course designed according to developmental principles. A sample of 165 students enrolled in the course participated in the study and was evaluated using the Measure of Epistemological Reflection and the Defining Issues Test. Findings indicate a positive movement from Perry's late dualistic stages to a multiplistic and early relativistic epistemology within the fourteen week semester. The authors encourage the use of concrete, and experiential activities drawing on multiple perspectives as well as knowledge sources.

Allen, W. R. 1992. The color of success: African-American college student outcomes at predominantly white and historically black public colleges and universities. *Harvard Educational Review* 62 (1): 26–44.

This study reports the findings of a survey conducted between 1981 and 1983 of over 2500 African American students at six predominantly white and eight historically black public colleges and universities (HBCUs). A number of variables relating to student educational background, demographics, educational aspirations, and institutional racial environment were examined in relation to outcomes of grade point average (GPA), future occupational goals, and social involvement with the campus. Students at HBCUs were found to have higher aspirations, better academic achievement as measured by GPA, and a higher level of social involvement with the campus relative to their counterparts at predominantly white institutions. The author stresses the need to understand the reasons behind HBCU success with African American students in order to translate it to other types of institutions.

Andreas, R. 1991. Where achievement is the rule: The case of Xavier University of Louisiana. In *The role and contribution of student affairs in involving colleges*, edited by G. Kuh and J. Schuh. San Francisco: Jossey-Bass.

The article examines Xavier University and its mission of excellence. The single most important point, the author finds, is that "members of the institution are moving in the same direction to attain the institution's purpose and student aspirations." The university's total devotion to the success of its students is revealed in its 60 percent graduation rate. One key to Xavier's success is a mentoring/student support program and an emphasis on the academic achievement and excellence of all students through "overcoming personal odds" and "bringing others along."

==

Andrew, L. D., and R. Russo. 1989. Who gets what?: Impact of financial aid policies. *Research in Higher Education* 30:471–483.

The authors analyze changes in federal financial aid programs as a result of the 1978, 1982, and 1986 amendments to the Higher Education Act and the resulting increases in the net costs of higher education to students. They find that the changes have had the greatest impact on low- and-middle income students and their options to choose the types of colleges and universities they will attend. The changes in financial aid and higher education funding have meant that African Americans and Latino/as in higher education are increasingly being directed to community colleges, which are less expensive and closer to their homes, and to proprietary institutions, which are very effective in communicating the positive outcomes of their programs.

==

Antony, J. 1993. Can we all get along?: How college impacts students' sense of the importance of promoting racial understanding. Paper presented at the annual meeting of the Association for the Study of Higher Education, November, at Pittsburgh, PA. ERIC, ED 365174.

This study, using data collected from 18,817 college students with the Cooperative Institutional Research Program's (CIRP) Freshman Survey, addresses the extent to which college affects students' sense of the importance of promoting racial understanding. Multiple regression analysis is used to study the manner in which various background characteristics, experiences, involvements, and college characteristics are related to attitudes toward diversity. Specifically, the development of this attitude is mediated by many variables that are independent of a student's race or any other background characteristics and are almost entirely dependent on the sorts of activities and courses he or she elects.

==

Asera, R., and P. U. Treisman. 1995. Routes to mathematics for African-American, Latino, and American Indian students in the 1990s: The educational trajectories of summer mathematics institute participants. In *Changing the culture: Mathematics education in the research community*, edited by N. D. Fisher, H. B. Keynes, and P. D. Wagreich. CBMS Issues in Mathematics Education, vol. 5. American Mathematical Society.

This report examines how students who are considering or are enrolled in advanced study in mathematics decided to pursue this path. The authors utilize retrospective interviews with 102 high-achieving African American, Latino/a, and American Indian students who participated in the 1989-1992 sessions of the Summer Mathematics Institute for Minority Undergraduates (SMI) held at Berkeley. Similarities among participants included support from family members to achieve academically, early achievement and interest in mathematics, high school teachers who demonstrated a personal interest in their success, and an affection for the objectivity of mathematics. In college, a faculty mentor and first-year honors math programs influenced many students to pursue math careers. Because many students are unaware of the career opportunities in math and often do not associate with other math students, the SMI provides an immersion experience in the mathematics community.

—

Association of American Colleges and Universities. 1995. *American pluralism and the college curriculum: Higher education in a diverse democracy.* Washington, DC.
The third in a series of reports issued as part of the AAC&U's American Commitments initiative, this publication makes specific recommendations for teaching diversity across the curriculum in both general education and major programs. The recommendations connect diversity with the study of both self and society, including the values of a democratic society. The report also describes effective diversity courses and requirements in a broad range of institutions, large and small, public and private, two-year and four-year. This publication is especially useful to members of curriculum and general education committees.

—

Astin, A. W. 1991. *Assessment for excellence: The philosophy and practice of assessment and evaluation in higher education.* New York: American Council on Education/Macmillan.
Astin proposes a new model for measuring excellence based on talent development. Rather than accepting the conventional view that an institution's quality can best be measured by its reputation and its resources, the author suggests a new approach to assessing excellence based on the role that institutions play in the growth and development of students as they move through the institution.

—

——. 1993a. Diversity and multiculturalism on campus: How are students affected? *Change* 25 (2): 44–49.
Astin uses data from the Higher Education Research Institute databases to examine questions of how institutional policies on diversity and multiculturalism, faculty emphasis on diversity, and direct involvement in "diversity experiences" influence various students. The author analyzes data on 25,000 students who entered college in the fall of 1985 and were followed-up four years later, as well as a data set on institutional commitment to diversity and multiculturalism. After controlling for entering student characteristics, Astin found that emphasis on institutional diversity is strongly associated with cultural awareness and commitment to promoting racial understanding, as well as with overall satisfaction with college. Similarly, emphasis on faculty diversity has positive effects on cultural awareness and overall satisfaction with college, and is associated with a greater tendency to vote in national elections. Courses in ethnic or women's studies and cultural awareness workshops show similar results. It is clear from the results that a strong emphasis on diversity in the institution and its faculty, and an opportunity for students to take courses on multicultural issues and to interact with others of different cultures, are all associated with outcomes considered positive in most general education programs.

—

——. 1993b. *What matters in college?: Four critical years revisited.* San Francisco: Jossey-Bass.

This massive study uses Astin's input-environment-outcome (I-E-O) model to assess the intellectual and social development and satisfaction with the college experience of over 20,000 students at 200 colleges and universities nationwide. The book examines the effects of 190 environmental variables on student personality, self-concept, attitudes, values, beliefs, patterns of behavior, academic and cognitive development, career development, and satisfaction with college. The chapter on student attitudes, values, and beliefs is of particular interest in the context of diversity research, as is the discussion of policy implications of the research.

====

Banta, T. W., ed. 1993. *Making a difference: Outcomes of a decade of assessment in higher education.* San Francisco: Jossey-Bass.

This volume contains twenty-three contributed papers on the subject of assessment in higher education, providing both a theoretical background and practical approaches to assessing the impact of particular programs. The papers are grouped along five major topic areas, including: "Transforming Campus Cultures Through Assessment;" "Adapting Assessment to Diverse Settings and Populations;" "Outcomes Assessment Methods that Work;" "Approaches with Promise for Improving Programs and Services;" and "State-Level Approaches to Assessment." There are extensive bibliographies and a summary section by the editor.

====

Bargad, A., and J. S. Hyde. 1991. Women's studies: A study of feminist identity development in women. *Psychology of Women Quarterly* 15:181–201.

This study investigates the effects of enrollment in an introductory women's studies course on women students' feminist identity. Researchers describe the creation and validation of a feminist identity scale created through factor analysis. Results of a survey using this scale and open-ended interviews revealed that the women's studies students experienced greater development in terms of the model than those in the control group. The authors conclude that women's studies courses have a positive influence on women students' sense of feminist identity.

====

Barnhardt, C. 1994. Life on the other side: Native student survival in a university world. *Peabody Journal of Education* 69 (2): 115–139.

From a literature review focused on developing a strategy to improve the academic success of American Indian students at the University of Alaska, Fairbanks' teacher education program, Barnhardt posits the characteristics of campuses where minority students have been academically successful as measured by GPA and retention. These institutions have: 1) mission statements that not only reflect, but celebrate diversity; 2) administrative involvement and support from campus leaders; 3) effective linkages with minority communities; 4) strong and numerous student support services available; 5) involvement of academic departments in minority issues; 6) active recruiting of minority faculty members and training, incentives, and rewards for all faculty for developing and using multicultural approaches in teaching and research; and 7) multicultural emphasis and opportunities for all students. While informal, this summary of the research provides insight into successful strategies for the retention and successes of American Indian and all minority students.

Beckham-Chasnoff, S. 1996. Homophobic attitude change. Ph.D. dissertation, Indiana
    State University, Terre Haute. Abstract in *Dissertation Abstracts International* 57
    (09): 5974B.
Using a sample of 128 students, the author measured the effect of a videotape containing educational and emotionally persuasive material on homophobia relative to a control video. Pre- to post-test scores for both groups showed no significant change in
homophobic attitudes for either video. The only significant increase in positive attitudes
was among students in the treatment video group who knew greater numbers of gays
and lesbians. Generally, higher levels of homophobia were found among men, students
from smaller hometowns, religiously conservative students, and those knowing fewer
gays and lesbians.

Beckenstein, L. 1992. Success rate of transfer students enrolled in a program for the
    underprepared at a senior college. *Journal of College Student Development* 33:56–60.
Beckenstein looks at factors that influence persistence to graduation and maintenance
of "good academic standing" among a cohort of 143 students who transferred into an
urban public university after completing their initial course work at a community college or another four-year institution. All of the students studied were participants in
various special programs for underprepared students at their original institutions and
became part of a similar program at the new institution. He finds the factors leading to
eventual success included number of credits brought to the new college and academic
success in the first term at the new college. Beckenstein suggests that in light of these
findings special orientation programs might be useful to increase the chances of success
of these transfer students.

Belgarde, W. L. 1992. The history of American Indian community colleges. In *ASHE*
    reader series: Racial and ethnic diversity in higher education, edited by C. Turner, M.
    García, A. Nora, and L. I. Rendon. Needham Heights, MA: Simon and Schuster.
The effectiveness of tribally-controlled community colleges (TCCCs) is explored in this
work. The experience of American Indians in higher education is examined with
emphasis on the development of TCCCs. The author maintains that these institutions
offer successful alternative means for educating American Indian students.

Bell, E. D., and R. W. Drakeford. 1992. A case study of the black student peer mentor
    program at the University of North Carolina–Greensboro in Fall 1987. *College*
    Student Journal 26:381–386.
This study examines the efficacy of an African American student peer mentor program
initiated by the University of North Carolina-Greensboro in fall 1987. Respondents
were given a survey instrument that measured autonomy, purpose, and interpersonal
relationships. Results indicate that participants in the mentor program were significantly less likely than those in the control group to drop out—all returned to the institution for their sophomore year. Peer mentor participants were also more likely than
non-participants to be involved in campus organizations and activities. Overall, the
peer mentor program helped its participants feel more connected to the university.

Benjamin, M. 1996. *Cultural diversity, educational equity, and the transformation of higher education: Group profiles as a guide to policy and programming.* Westport, CT: Praeger.

This book has three major sections. The first introduces the idea of cultural diversity as it applies to higher education. The second section contains four ethnic profiles on African Americans, Latino/as, Asian Americans, and Jews. Each profile centers on students in the context of their group through the following categories: context and history, modal social class, definition of the family, life cycle, husband-wife relations, parent-child relations, perspectives on help-seeking, and a summary perspective on each group. In the final section, a discussion on the connection between policy actions and diversity objectives leads to eight principles that apply to all participants in the institution. Employing the information from the profiles about student background and behavior, Benjamin explores the efficacy of many areas of university functioning, including access and enrollment, financial aid, student services, and student orientation.

======

Bennett, C., and A. M. Okinaka. 1990. Factors related to persistence among Asian, black, Hispanic, and white undergraduates at a predominantly white university: Comparison between first and fourth year cohorts. *Urban Review* 22 (1): 33–60.

The authors conducted a follow-up study on attrition for undergraduate students at Indiana University. They link the high attrition rates among African Americans, Latino/as, and American Indians on campus to the poor campus climate that existed for students of color. Even Asian American students, who had a higher retention rate, felt alienated by the campus environment. European American students and Latino/a students who were least satisfied and felt the most alienated dropped out. African American and Asian American students who persisted to their fourth year on campus felt less satisfied and more socially alienated than students from these groups who had left.

======

Benns-Suter, R. 1993. *The utilization of simulations in multicultural education.* Millersville, PA: Millersville University. ERIC, ED 364613.

In a counseling course designed to prepare students to function effectively in a pluralistic society, early results suggest that while students were able to comprehend underlying theory, they had difficulty grasping issues related to racial and cultural differences. The use of simulation methods was found to be effective in stimulating thinking about the issues.

======

Bensimon, E. 1995a. *African-Americans and Jews: The disuniting of a model urban campus.* University Park: Pennsylvania State University.

This critical case study unveils the bias of taken-for-granted beliefs about innovation and change in a public urban college by contrasting the view of organizational elites to the view of those outside the center of power. This is accomplished by an examination of a bitter confrontation that turned Jewish and African American faculty, administrators, and students against one another. This case study shows how a grant designed to enhance teaching and learning environments actually served to entrench long-term organizational structures and practices that contributed to the disuniting of what had been described as a model campus.

——. 1995b. *Creating an institutional identity out of differences: A case study of multicultural organizational change.* University Park: Pennsylvania State University.
This case study examines the efforts of a college to exchange an organizational structure that is monocultural for one that is grounded in the racial diversity of the student body. The paper details organizational changes that occurred at the institution between 1987 and 1991 and presents the results of interviews with faculty, administrators, students, and trustees. Analysis of the case study indicates that leadership was an organizational characteristic crucial to the institution's transformation, that a new mission statement had a significant effect, as did the appointment of women and minorities to the president's cabinet. Also affecting the institution's transformation was the appointment of African Americans and Latino/as to the faculty and a commitment to multicultural curricular transformation.

====

——, ed. 1994. *Multicultural teaching and learning: Strategies for change in higher education.* University Park: Pennsylvania State University.
This edited volume is a sourcebook of readings focused on conceptual issues for framing approaches to a multicultural curriculum and models for achieving curricular change.

====

Bevis, T. B. 1997. Language partners. *About Campus* 2 (2): 23–24.
A long-term program at the University of Arkansas linked international students with native English speakers as a method for international students to improve their English language skills. An unintended side effect of the program was a reported increase in understanding of and appreciation for diversity by the native English speakers. Recently the program was applied more broadly in a geography class when the instructor wanted students to develop an understanding of culture as well as physical geography. Over 90 percent of the geography students participated in the program. Some chose to continue to participate in the language program and many of the international students encouraged other international students to participate. Students reported that they valued learning about other cultures and recognized the importance of diversity. Some students are including such study in their curricular and extracurricular activities.

====

Bidell, T. R., E. M. Lee, N. Bouchie, C. Ward, and D. Brass. 1994. Developing conceptions of racism among young white adults in the context of cultural diversity coursework. Paper presented at the annual meeting of the American Educational Research Association, April, at New Orleans, LA. ERIC, ED 377270.
This is an exploratory study designed to determine if white students enrolled in a college cultural diversity course would develop a deeper understanding of racism. Fifty-five white students in a course required for education majors showed a deepening of their understandings of racism.

====

Bonsangue, M. V., and D. E. Drew. 1995. Increasing minority students' success in calculus. In *Fostering student success in quantitative gateway courses*, edited by J. Gainen and E. W. Willemsen. New Directions for Teaching and Learning, no. 61. San Francisco: Jossey-Bass.

This five-year study focuses on the effects of the Academic Excellence Workshop programs in chemistry, physics, and mechanical engineering on 133 Latino/a and African American students who attended at least one calculus workshop while enrolled in a traditional lecture course in these areas. This group was compared to 187 African American and Latino/a, 28 European American, and 198 Asian American or Pacific Islander students who were not enrolled in the workshop. Fifty percent of the non-workshop participants left the institution in three years, while only 15 percent of the workshop participants left. Ninety-one percent of the workshop students continued in the field of science, math, or engineering, as compared to 58 percent of the non-workshop participants who dropped out of math and science related courses. The completion rate for African American and Latino/a students in the workshop was 91 percent, as compared to 82 percent of the white students and 89 percent for Asian American students of the non-workshop group.

===

Bowser, B. P., T. Jones, and G. A. Young. 1993. *Confronting diversity issues on campus.* Newbury Park, CA: Sage.
This book presents a practical approach to how the institution, its administrators, faculty, and students respond to racism and unequal power relationships. An important distinction is made between the official organization and the "unwritten organization" which is "the murky underground of the informal structure of the university." The organizational knowledge and insight are informed by clear examples. In addition, four current issues are discussed: the purpose of education; affirmative action; freedom of speech; and the role of ethnic studies. A number of strategies and suggestions for programs are given using case studies, sample interactions, and diversity stories.

===

———. 1995. *Toward the multicultural university.* Westport, CT: Praeger.
This book contains three sections. The first provides important historical, statistical, and conceptual frameworks for thinking about multicultural universities. The second profiles the challenges facing Puerto Rican, Latino/a, and American Indian populations of students. The third section focuses on concrete suggestions for developing a multicultural institution.

===

Boyer, P. 1997. *Native American colleges: Progress and prospects.* Princeton, NJ: Carnegie Foundation for the Advancement of Teaching.
This report on the current status of tribally-controlled community colleges is based on a three month site visit to a single campus, a national survey of 1600 tribal college students, available research, and discussions with educators and leaders nationwide. The study documents the continuing development of tribal colleges, evidence of positive impact on students, and contributions to local economies and communities. The study reveals lower unemployment rates among graduates, higher aspirations of students and communities, and a revival of cultural traditions. Success appears related to culturally compatible educational environments, ease of access, education about American Indian history and culture, links to communities, and pedagogy which believes in student success and capabilities. In order to reduce the levels of contrast between the Indian and non-Indian educational systems, the author urges that American Indian history, traditions, and governance be included throughout U. S. education.

Bradley, J., R. Philippi, and J. Bryant. 1992. Minorities benefit from their association with campus recreation programs. *NIRSA Journal* 16 (3): 46–50.

Two thousand students, of whom 10 percent were minorities, were surveyed by the Center for Assessment Research and Development and the National Intramural-Recreational Sports Association to learn about the importance of recreational services to minority students. Results indicate that approximately 90 percent of all minorities responding to the survey participate in recreation each week, with the majority participating at least three times per week. Minority responses to the importance of recreational facilities and programs for their decision to attend and continue at their chosen university suggest that minority students are more likely than their white counterparts to rank recreation programs as important to very important. Results also imply that campus recreation programs play an important role in the integration of students into the institutional environment.

Brown, L. L., and S. E. R. Kurpius. 1997. Psychosocial factors influencing academic persistence of American Indian college students. *Journal of College Student Development* 38 (1): 3–12.

The authors, using Tinto's model of attrition, surveyed 288 of the 378 American Indian undergraduates attending a large Southwestern university to identify factors contributing to persistence in college. Five years later, 149 had graduated or were still enrolled in college; 139 were classified as non-persisters. Persisters reported significantly higher degree aspirations and better high school preparation, higher GPAs, and had assimilated academic norms of good study habits and regular class attendance. Persisters also reported higher and more positive interactions with faculty and staff. No differences were found in perceived discrimination, social integration, family encouragement, or the valuing of education.

California Postsecondary Education Commission. 1990. *Toward an understanding of campus climate: A report to the Legislature in response to Assembly Bill 4071.* Commission Report no. 90-19. Sacramento, CA. ERIC, ED 329202.

In 1988 the California Legislature directed the state's Postsecondary Education Commission to conduct a feasibility study on assessing the current state of the campus climate for diversity across all four segments of higher education in that state (community colleges, the California State University, the University of California, and independent colleges and universities). The report contains an extensive discussion of the use of focus groups to assess climate issues, as well as other methods to determine the current state and to measure changes in climate. Included as an appendix is a report on differential treatment of various groups in higher education prepared by the University of California Student Association.

———. 1992. *Resource guide for assessing campus climate.* Commission Report no. 92-24. Sacramento, CA.

A very useful guide for practitioners interested in studying campus climate, this resource includes descriptions of over fifty studies of campus climate, most conducted at the institutional level. The bulk of the studies cited are surveys, grouped into three areas based on the populations surveyed. These groups include: current students, former students, faculty, staff, and other participants. The guide also includes pools of survey items on various topics related to campus climate for those developing their own climate surveys.

===

Capoor, M., and D. Overstreet. 1993. Assessment of multiple treatments used to help underprepared students. Paper presented at the annual meeting of the Association for Institutional Research, May, at Chicago, IL.

Capoor and Overstreet tracked 11,758 students in the 1986-1900 fall entering cohorts at Middlesex Community College in New Jersey. Student outcomes (persistence and GPA) for students participating in eight programs designed to assist high-risk and underprepared students with the transition to college were evaluated. The programs ranged from basic skills development to ESL programs to counseling and social services for reentry students. The results show that tutoring and basic skills instruction were most strongly associated with both measures of success, while a college survival course, taken with no other interventions, was least strongly associated with success. Also included in this study is the evaluation of a program for students with physical and mental disabilities. Students in this program of evaluation, counseling, tutoring, and accommodation were found to have the highest rate of success on the two indicators used in the study.

===

Carnegie Foundation for the Advancement of Teaching. 1989. *Tribal colleges: Shaping the future of Native America. A special report.* Lawrenceville, NJ: Princeton University Press.

This report is a frequently cited watershed in the recognition of the development of trib-ally-controlled colleges from their beginnings in the late 1960s. Written by Paul Boyer, the report outlines the four characteristics common to each campus which help ensure the success of American Indian students. First, they establish a learning environment which encourages participation and builds the self-confidence of students who expect to fail. Second, tribal colleges celebrate and sustain American Indian traditions. Third, they provide essential community services. Finally, they serve as centers of research and scholarship on American Indian concerns.

===

Carter, D. F. 1997. A dream deferred? Examining the degree aspirations of African Americans and white college students. Ph.D. dissertation, University of Michigan.

Examining national data, Carter finds that the percentage of African American enroll-ment in a college—a diversity indicator—has significant positive effects on African American degree aspirations during college, even after controlling for initial aspira-tions, background, and other college experiences.

===

Castle, E. 1993. Minority student attrition research: Higher education's challenge for human resource development. *Educational Researcher* 22 (7): 24–30.

This article addresses higher education's challenge to enroll and retain to graduation ethnic minorities, especially African Americans and Latino/as. Suggestions are made for institutional research on minority attrition that is focused, context and group spe-cific, and longitudinal. The author also suggests that minority faculty and administra-tors be included in the research. The first section focuses on the relationship between student life, human development needs, and problems with the underrepresentation of minorities in higher education and the skilled labor force. The second section calls for more effective research on attrition and the disparity between future job opportunities and cognitive skill levels. The third section warns predominantly white institutions against basing intervention methods upon research that is not in the best interest of the minority student population.

═══

Caston, J. J. 1994. The learning experience: Impact on measures of institutional effectiveness. Paper presented at "Leadership 2000," the annual international conference of the League for Innovation in the Community College and the Community College Leadership Program, July, at San Diego, CA. ERIC, ED 375907.

In 1994, a study was administered at Cosumnes River College in California. Instructors used computer-assisted instruction and student-centered discussions or lectures. The findings showed that students were more likely to attend lectures if they were twenty-five or older, European American and female, or a native English speaker. Students of color, those under twenty-five years of age, or European American men earned higher grades in the "mixed repertoire" courses. All students thought they had a better chance of doing well in courses with lectures.

═══

Chambers, T., and J. Lewis. 1992. A two-dimensional approach to understanding cultural differences and discrimination: A workshop within a workshop. *Journal of College Student Development* 33:79–81.

This article describes a cultural differences workshop conducted as part of a larger leadership series at a Midwestern university. Participants were told they were participating in a workshop on diversity, but in addition to the workshop that they expected, they were divided into two groups. One group was treated throughout the workshop as privileged while the other was subject to a variety of discriminatory actions. At the end of the workshop a discussion allowed all participants to discuss their reactions to the discrimination within the workshop itself and how they might use the experience to better understand broader instances of discrimination in the university and the world. Participant reports suggest the effectiveness of the model in developing cultural sensitivity.

═══

Chan, K. S., and S. Hune. 1995. Racialization and pan-ethnicity: From Asians in America to Asian Americans. In *Toward a common destiny: Improving race and ethnic relations in America*, edited by W. D. Hawley and A. W. Jackson. San Francisco: Jossey-Bass.

This chapter is an important treatment of theories of racial identity formation in the context of the Asian American experience in America. The authors take an empirical look at anti-Asian and Asian American violence, the "model minority" myth, the complexity within the Asian American community, and the evidence and disparities in educational and economic attainment.

═══

Chan, K. S., and L. C. Wang. 1991. Racism and the model minority: Asian Americans in higher education. In *The racial crisis in American higher education*, edited by P. G. Altbach and K. Lomotey. New York: State University of New York Press.

The authors analyze structure and power on U. S. college campuses, using as case studies current situations of Asian American studies programs and efforts to limit Asian American admissions to some elite institutions. The authors note that although the most public issues around race in higher education have generally centered on African Americans, other minority groups also face the challenges of racism.

===

Chang, M. J. 1996. Racial diversity in higher education: Does a racially mixed student population affect educational outcomes? Ph.D. dissertation, University of California, Los Angeles. Abstract in *Dissertation Abstracts International* 57 (04): 1513A.

Using the 1985 Cooperative Institutional Research Program survey of college freshmen and the 1989 follow-up, this study looked at the impact of different levels of racial diversity at 300 colleges and universities. The sample included 11,600 students. To quantify the racial diversity at each institution, the researcher developed measures to identify opportunities for cross-racial interaction. The author found that, in general, environmental and experiential components of a diverse campus have positive impacts on retention, overall college satisfaction, college GPA, and intellectual and social self-confidence. There is some indication that campus racial diversity has a negative effect on, or does not enhance the experiences, of some aspects of the college experience of students of color. This broad research on the effects of a diverse student population on student outcomes may be especially useful in this time of attacks on affirmative action programs as a way to make student populations more diverse.

===

Chavez, R. C., J. O'Donnell, and R. L. Gallegos. 1994. Pre-service students' perspectives on "dilemmas" in a multicultural education course. Paper presented at the annual meeting of the American Educational Research Association, April, at New Orleans, LA. ERIC, ED 370917.

This study was designed to assess the impact of a required multicultural education course on undergraduate education majors at New Mexico State University. The assessment itself involved gathering pre- and post-course information to determine students' ideas and attitudes about multicultural issues. At the beginning of the semester, participants (n = 65) were presented with a "dilemma" involving an inappropriate representation of American Indians in sporting events and were asked to write their reactions. Researchers conducted content analyses of the pre- and post-course essays and concluded that there was no significant change in students' evaluation of the dilemmas between measures. In other words, students entered the course with attitudes that largely reflected the racial status quo and, for the most part, left the course with the same beliefs. Researchers hypothesized that the course had no effect because it failed to confront three knowledge domains: the personal, the historical, and the ideological and cultural.

===

Chen, S. 1995. On the ethnic studies requirement. In *The Asian American educational experience*. Edited by D. T. Nakanishi and T. Y. Nishida. New York: Routledge.

This article describes the authors' experiences teaching diversity courses in a variety of settings and in classes with varied demographics. The author found benefits to the experience of classroom diversity in an Asian American studies courses, although there was negative impact on Asian American students' participation when classes became predominantly white.

Chesler, M. A., and X. Zúñiga. 1991. Dealing with prejudice and conflict in the classroom: The pink triangle exercise. *Teaching Sociology* 19:173–181.

The reactions of twenty-five students to an exercise for their "Intergroup Conflict and
Social Change" class were examined. Students were asked to wear a pink triangle, a
symbol for homosexuality, during one full day on campus. The authors used students'
decisions to wear or not to wear the button and descriptions of others' reactions as
material for experiential learning. Excerpts of students' experiences recorded in papers
are used to demonstrate increased understanding of stigma, personal identity, internal-
ized oppression, public identity, social conformity, anticipation of rejection, and the tension between personal identity and political values.

===

Childers, M. 1997. -Ism (n.): Lessons learned from the National Video Diversity
Project. *Change* 29 (2): 33–37.

This article communicates the preliminary results and experiences of a project funded
by the Institute for Public Media Arts designed to teach about diversity using the video
documentary process. It involved a group of thirty-three professors, video artists, counselors, administrators, and community organizers from eleven different colleges and
universities. The goal of the project was to use a video documentary process to help
students become reflective about their attitudes towards diversity and, in the process,
create public dialogue to improve student relations. Some of the positive outcomes of
the project include: interest between cultures generated by video diaries; the ability of
students to speak more openly about their experiences and reservations; and the opportunity to learn about each other in a personal and academic setting. Overall, the project is intended to show that teaching and learning might occur at the same time for
students and faculty in ways required for multicultural teaching.

===

Christensen, S., and L. M. Sorenson. 1994. Effects of a multi-factor education program
on the attitude of child and youth worker students toward gays and lesbians. *Child
and Youth Care Forum* 23 (2): 119–233.

This research reports on attempts to ameliorate the negative attitudes of counseling
students who work with gay and lesbian youth. Often caregivers' attitudes are negative
and negatively impact clients. The students showed some improved attitudes over a
period of time in two post-tests.

===

Clewell, B. C., and M. S. Ficklen. 1986. *Improving minority retention in higher education:
A search for effective institutional practices.* Princeton, NJ: Educational Testing
Service. ERIC, ED 299841.

Retention programs for minority students at four predominantly white institutions
were examined through case studies. The four institutions, Boston College, California
State University at Fresno, Purdue University (minority engineering programs), and
the University of North Carolina at Greensboro, were identified through an analysis
of retention data reported to the College Board and through a peer nomination process.
Although there was great variation among programs, key elements of a successful
retention effort were identified. These included establishing institutional policies to
enhance minority student retention, demonstrating an institutional commitment to
minority student success, institutionalizing the program, establishing an institutional
climate which is inclusive, providing comprehensive services through dedicated staff,

performing adequate data collection and follow-up, and ensuring faculty support for the program and non-stigmatization of the participants. An appendix consisting of the four case study reports is included.

———

Collier, L. 1993. Teaching Native students at the college level. *Canadian Journal of Native Education* 20 (1): 109–117.

Collier relates the case of a class she taught with older American Indian students through a nursing program at John Abbot College in Quebec, Canada. After reading literature on the learning styles of American Indians and her experience with students in her class, Collier recommends never putting American Indian students on the spot in class, providing more small group work, encouraging laughter as an appropriate response in some situations, and taking the time to develop a personal relationship with American Indian students. Specific outcomes based on the class are not reported.

———

Conciatore, J. 1990. From flunking to mastering calculus: Treisman's retention model proves to be "too good" on some campuses. *Black Issues in Higher Education* 6 (22): 5–6.

This article presents the results of a study conducted by University of California, Berkeley faculty member Uri Treisman that explores the causes of poor performance in and difficulty with calculus among minority students. Following a survey of 1,000 faculty members at Berkeley and interviews with minority students and their families, Treisman found that many minority students were academic loners struggling one-on-one with a subject that 300,000 out of 600,000 students fail each year. Following the development and implementation of a learning community program to enhance retention, grades have increased and attrition has decreased. The program has been adopted at more than twenty-five institutions since its initial implementation at Berkeley.

———

Corley, T. J., and R. H. Pollack. 1996. Do changes in the stereotypic depiction of a lesbian couple affect heterosexuals' attitudes toward lesbianism? *Journal of Homosexuality* 32 (2): 1–17.

This study measured the effect of an educational treatment in an introductory psychology class of seventy-eight heterosexual women and sixty-three heterosexual men, with a mean age of nineteen years. Men with higher traditional sex role values showed significantly more positive attitudes toward lesbians after they read a non-stereotypical description of a lesbian couple (both partners displaying feminine characteristics). Men with lower traditional sex role values showed no difference in attitudes after reading descriptions of two feminine, two masculine, and a masculine and feminine lesbian couple. Women with higher and lower traditional sex role values did not differ significantly in their attitudes toward lesbians after the treatment. The study suggests that men who hold traditional sex role orientations may become more positive toward lesbians if they are presented in a way that does not violate gender roles.

———

Cornwell, G. H., and E. Stoddard. 1996. Residential colleges: Laboratories for teaching through difference. In *Democratic education in an age of difference: Redefining citizenship in higher education*, edited by R. Guarasci and G. H. Cornwell. San Francisco: Jossey-Bass.

This chapter contains a review of some of the research examining the benefits of separate education for students of color and women. It also describes a residential learning experience in terms of design and its impact on students.

====

Cross, K. P. 1974. *Beyond the open door: New students in higher education.* San Francisco: Jossey-Bass.

In this classic text which traces the history of "new" students in American higher education, Cross presents the results of studying various groups of new students (first generation college students, minority students, women, educationally disadvantaged). Her work laid the groundwork for the past two decades of studies on various student populations and their experience and expectations of educational environments. In a significant chapter, "The Threat of Failure," she discusses the fact that students who are in significant academic jeopardy often compound their difficulties by not seeking academic help or seeking it too late. Their lack of realistic assessment of the educational requirements and of their own preparation often leads to the paradox that they don't recognize the need to seek help until it is too late. The data clearly demonstrate that this phenomenon is true of both majority and minority students who meet the criteria for being called "new" students.

====

Cross, T. L. 1993. The myth that preferential college admissions create high African American student dropout rates. *Journal of Blacks in Higher Education* 1 (1): 71–74.

Critics of affirmative action in university admissions frequently suggest that admitting minority students based on differential criteria is unfair in that they will lack the skills needed to succeed in college and therefore become dropouts rather than graduates. Cross takes issue with this assertion by examining African American student retention rates nationwide using data from the NCAA and *Peterson's Guide to Four-Year Colleges.* He found that, nationally, African American college students had a graduation rate of approximately 56 percent. The highest African American graduation rates were found at highly selective liberal arts institutions and universities with strong affirmative action policies. Less selective state universities showed much lower graduation rates. While the study does not control for several confounding variables such as selectivity, it does suggest that students admitted under affirmative action programs do prosper at those institutions with a strong commitment to such programs, while students who enroll at less selective state institutions do not fare as well.

====

Croteau, J. M., and M. T. Kusek. 1992. Gay and lesbian speaker panels: Implementation and research. *Journal of Counseling and Development* 70:396–401.

This definitive research review gathers available literature on the use of personal stories and question and answer periods with lesbians and gays to decrease anti-homosexual attitudes. All of the published studies reported favorable effects using lesbian and gay speaker panels, though the authors recommend further evaluation of specific aspects of these panels and the use of control groups and random assignment for comparison. An excellent reference list is included.

====

Curtis, D. E., and J. Heritage. 1991. Influencing homonegative attitudes in college students through an educational unit on homosexuality. Paper presented at the meeting of the Middle Tennessee Psychological Association, April, at Nashville, TN. ERIC, ED 346388.

This study found that seventy-five students in a class entitled "Psychosexual Development" reported significantly more positive attitudes toward homosexuals than a control group after a unit on homosexuality. The unit included films, a book chapter, a pamphlet on homosexuality and Christianity, and a lecture by an ordained minister who was non-stereotypically gay. Students who had a lesbian or gay friend demonstrated the least homonegativity.

Darder, A. 1991. *Culture and power in the classroom: A critical foundation for bicultural education.* New York: Bergin and Garvey.

This book examines, through the use of critical theory, the relationships of power and dominance experienced in the educational process by students who are not of the dominant culture. It addresses the concept of biculturalism, where individuals learn to become functional not only in the primary culture of their home and community, but in the dominant (mainstream) culture as well. Critical educational practices and emancipatory classroom projects, such as a bicultural development program at Pacific Oaks College in California, are profiled through a review of student reactions.

D'Augelli, A. R., and S. L. Hershberger. 1993. African American undergraduates on a predominantly white campus: Academic factors, social networks, and campus climate. *Journal of Negro Education* 62 (1): 67–79.

This study, modeled on Tinto's theory, highlights the experiences of African American students on a large, predominantly white university campus located in a rural area several hours from most of its African American students' homes. A total of 146 paired undergraduate students, 73 African American and 73 white, at a large mid-Atlantic state university participated in the study. All student pairs had grade point averages within one quarter point of each other. The survey instrument contained sections relating to demographics, frequency and impact of student life events, minority personal contacts, and social support networks. There were major differences in the racial compositions of the paired students' high schools. African American fathers had less education and their family income was less than their white counterparts. Minimal differences were reported in terms of family support for being enrolled as a student. The study also found that African American students' social networks contained significantly fewer people who were college or university graduates and this was directly related to the students' support for attending the university. There was no significant difference in campus involvement between the two groups. The findings of this study revealed that the African American students' experiences on this campus reflect the aspects of their personal backgrounds that differ from those of whites more than they reflect differences in academic backgrounds. Minor differences were noted in the African American students' experiences on campus, but they were more troubled by the events they experienced, thus reporting lower well-being. There was no evidence that the climate for African American students hindered their academic success. Racial discrimination was the only discernable difference noted between the two groups which was directly related to the African American students' lower overall satisfaction with campus life.

Davine, V. R. 1994. Multicultural instruction and attitude change. Ph.D. dissertation,
University of Iowa. Abstract in *Dissertation Abstracts International* 55 (12): 3767A.
This study surveys 342 students enrolled in a required teacher education course that
focuses on diversity issues at the University of Iowa. The goal of the study is to assess
the impact of the course on the students' attitudes about affirmative action, increasing
diversity on their campus, and other diversity issues. This study utilizes a pre- and post-
test design to assess the impact of the course. The results indicate that, in general, the
course affected student attitudes in the desired direction. However, the pattern of
change was not the same for all attitude statements. Attitude change was not related to
the instructor, semester, or student background characteristics. The course's long-term
impact was not assessed.

===

Davis, J. 1992. Factors contributing to post-secondary achievement of American
Indians. *Tribal College* 4 (2): 24–30.
Davis used the case studies of ten American Indian college graduates to identify family and educational characteristics impacting their success. The students attended public, private, two-year, four-year, and tribal colleges. In seven of the cases, graduates
attributed their success to encouragement from a particular family member. They also
cited a personal desire for betterment.

===

Davis, L. E., and J. S. Turner. 1993. An investigation of the cultural sensitivity level of
elementary pre-service teachers. Paper presented at the annual meeting of the
Mid-South Educational Research Association, November, at New Orleans, LA.
ERIC, ED 372054.
This study is a multi-institutional analysis of the level of cultural diversity awareness
of elementary pre-service teachers enrolled in Southern universities accredited by the
National Council for the Accreditation of Teacher Education (NCATE). A random
sample of respondents was administered the Cultural Diversity Awareness Inventory.
The results indicate that subjects exhibited cultural sensitivity in the areas of the culturally diverse family, cross-cultural communication, and the creation of a multicultural environment using multicultural methods and materials. No statistically
significant differences were found based on participation in a multicultural education
course, race, or prior high school attendance at a private, public, or parochial institution. The authors conclude that teacher education programs in the South appear to be
preparing pre-service teachers to be culturally sensitive and that separate multicultural courses added to the curriculum may be unnecessary.

===

Delphin, M., and D. Rollock. 1995. University alienation and African American ethnic identity as predictors of attitudes toward, knowledge about, and likely use of
psychological services. *Journal of College Student Development* 36:337–346.
This article describes a study that examined the relationship between the racial identity attitudes of African American male students and their rate of student involvement.
From a total of 900 surveys sent to ten predominantly white universities in the
Southeastern United States, a total of 117 African American males completed and
returned the instrument. Students were asked to complete the Student Involvement
Survey (SIS), the Racial Identity Attitudes Scale (RIAS-B), and provide demograph-
ic data. Greek affiliation was the only demographic variable found to contribute signif-

icantly to total student involvement and racial identity attitudes. The study also supported the hypothesis that relationships exist between the racial identity attitudes of African American male students and their rate of student involvement. The article encourages student affairs professionals to recognize the importance of cultural identity development to retention of African American male students.

━━

Deltz, R. 1992. A blueprint for Hispanic student success. *Outlook in Higher Education* 2 (10): 5–8.

This article looks at Madonna College and its success in retaining undergraduate disadvantaged and culturally diverse students. The institution's blueprint was very clear: to do whatever necessary to insure students were successful in fulfilling their academic obligations. Through the Office of Multicultural Affairs, minority students were given academic, financial, motivational, and personal assistance. The key to Madonna's success was the personal attention and individual care given students.

━━

DeSousa, J. D., and P. King. 1992. Are white students really more involved in collegiate experiences than black students? *Journal of College Student Development* 33:263–269.

DeSousa and King look at one of the myths of student involvement—that because of a poor fit between African American students and predominantly white institutions, African American students are likely to be less involved and active in various kinds of college activities, both intellectual/academic and social/interpersonal. The College Student Experience Questionnaire was administered to a randomly selected sample of African American and white students at a large Midwestern university. Responses to the questionnaire reveal that African American students were more involved in a variety of activities, both intellectual/academic and social/interpersonal. This research, although based on only one institution, raises interesting questions about the conventional wisdom on African American students at predominantly white colleges and universities.

━━

DeSousa, J. D., and G. Kuh. 1996. Does institutional racial composition make a difference in what black students gain from college? *Journal of College Student Development* 37:257–267.

The authors looked at African American students at one historically black institution and one predominantly white institution to determine if the time invested in college experiences differed by institutional type, if there were differences in the educational gains of students at the different kinds of institutions, and what types of participation influenced the educational gains of students. The research used the College Student Experiences Questionnaire and compared the differences in mean scores of students at each type of institution. Students at the historically African American institution devoted greater effort to academic activities and indicated greater gains in personal and social development, critical thinking and science/technology, vocational and career skills, history and cultural awareness, and arts and literature. Based on student reports, different kinds of activities had differential impacts on student gains depending on the type of institution. The discoveries of this research suggest that greater exchanges between historically black institutions and predominantly white institutions—which influence different kinds of success by African American students—would be worthwhile.

=

Dodd, J., F. Garcia, C. Meccage, and R. Nelson. 1995. American Indian student retention. *NASPA Journal* 33:72–79.

This study examines and identifies factors contributing to the success of American Indian students at a college or university. The academically successful American Indian students were older adults and married or formerly married students. Also, American Indian students experienced racism and overcame it because of their strong tribal affiliation. Their high school teachers played an important role in encouraging these students throughout high school.

=

Drew, D. 1996. *Aptitude revisited: Rethinking math and science education for America's next century.* Baltimore: The Johns Hopkins University Press.

Taking the view that quality education in mathematics and science is vital for the people who will make up U. S. society in the future, Drew looks at the current state of mathematics and science education at all levels. Rather than accept the conventional wisdom about aptitude for mathematics or science, Drew identifies approaches to change mathematics and science education so that students can succeed.

=

Durham, R., J. Hays, and R. Martinez. 1994. Socio-cognitive development among Chicano and Anglo American college students. *Journal of College Student Development* 35:178–182.

Using essays designed to assess socio-cognitive development according to the Perry scheme, the researchers compared the performance of groups of white and Chicano students. The socio-economic background of the Chicano students was also assessed to determine if it had any impact on performance. Blinded holistic writing assessments were also conducted by trained writing evaluators. Correlations between age, gender, class, holistic writing score, and Perry level were run. For Chicanos the only significant correlation was between holistic writing score and Perry level. For white students there were multiple significant correlations, including age to holistic writing score (negative), class level to Perry score, and class level to holistic writing score. Past research suggests that year in college and age contribute to Perry score, but for Chicano students in this study the correlations were negative or approached zero. This research suggests that intellectual performance measured by the Perry score is independent of the college academic experience. The pattern of correlations identified in this study may have significant implications for how colleges and universities approach the education of Chicano students. The models practiced for white students may need to be reevaluated in light of student experiences.

=

Duster, T. 1993. The diversity of the University of California at Berkeley: An emerging reformulation of competence in an increasingly multicultural world. In *Beyond a dream deferred: Multicultural education and the politics of excellence*, edited by B. W. Thompson and S. Tyagi. Minneapolis: University of Minnesota Press.

This chapter suggests that a reformulation of patterns of student integration be conceptualized which focuses on a complex relationship between identity enhancing activities and student interactions across race and ethnicity. The analysis is based on an important and in-depth study of student interaction at the University of California—Berkeley.

≡

Faison, J. 1993. Unmeasured but essential: Distinguishing factors between African American graduate school persisters and non-persisters. Ph.D. dissertation. Emory University.
This quantitative and qualitative study identifies factors that distinguish African Americans who successfully earn graduate degrees from predominantly white institutions from those who do not. Faison examines mentor support, university climate, student networks, student support services, department climate, and university climate.

≡

———. 1996. The next generation: The mentoring of African American graduate students on predominantly white university campuses. Paper presented at the annual meeting of the American Education Research Association, New York.
This in-depth qualitative study identifies behaviors exhibited by mentors of African American doctoral students at predominantly white universities that contribute to the success of their mentoring relationship. Participants discuss significant characteristics and behaviors of successful mentors of African American graduate students at predominantly white institutions and discuss what made these relationships work.

≡

Falk, D., and L. P. Aitken. 1984. Promoting retention among American Indian college students. *Journal of American Indian Education* 23 (2): 24–31.
Falk and Aitken report that 69 percent of educators in their survey thought American Indian studies programs are important or very important in improving American Indian retention. A significant relationship between attendance at American Indian student organization meetings and retention was also found.

≡

Farley, J. E. 1995. *Majority-minority relations.* 3d ed. Englewood Cliffs, NJ: Prentice-Hall.
This is a comprehensive, current reference on majority-minority group relations. Specific sections deal with hate speech, classes on diversity, and exercises to reduce prejudice.

≡

Fischer, B., and D. Hartmann. 1995. The impact of race on the social experience of college students at a predominantly white university. *Journal of Black Studies* 26 (2): 117–133.
In 1991, Southwest Missouri State University initiated a study regarding the quality of African American students' overall social experience on a predominantly white campus. The study explored the importance of making friends of other ethnicities. Of the 102 African American students, 74 percent stated that interracial friendships would enhance learning, while 18 percent said it increased their potential for adjustment on the predominantly white campus and their potential for success. Percentages for white students were not mentioned. The study noted that a student's social life and opportunities are strongly affected by his/her racial background. Seventy-four percent of African American students and 51 percent of white students stated there was a need for better interracial relations on campus. The study found that students will not associate with individuals if they do not wish to, thereby suggesting that the university is

only partially responsible for the racial conflicts on campus. The data indicated that minorities are reminded daily that they are a minority and consequently feel alienated from campus life. Students offered suggestions for improving interracial relations on campus. Sixty percent of whites and 67 percent of African Americans requested opportunities involving more interracial interaction, communication, and activities. Students also suggested having seminars and lectures about racial prejudice.

===

Fleming, J. 1985. *Blacks in college: A comparative study of students' success in black and white institutions.* San Francisco: Jossey-Bass. ERIC, ED 266745.

This book presents the results of a major study of the experience of African American students at white and historically black colleges and universities. The study looks at student experiences in terms of achievement, cognitive development, and student backgrounds, including gender. Fleming's results present powerful evidence of the importance of campus climate, involvement in campus life, interaction with faculty, and expectations for success—conditions more likely to be found at the historically black institutions.

===

Francis, P. L. 1993. Assessing the effectiveness of multicultural curriculum initiatives in higher education: Proving the self-evident. In *Strategies for implementation in colleges and universities,* edited by J. Q. Adams and J. R. Welsch. Multicultural Education, vol. 3. Macomb, IL: Western Illinois University.

This article reviews the research literature pertaining to the assessment of multicultural curriculum initiatives—at the single course level, as well as at the broader, programmatic level. In general, the author asserts that there is little but anecdotal and descriptive evidence available to demonstrate the effectiveness of these curricular initiatives. Because of the lack of studies assessing the effects of multicultural curriculum changes, and because of the existence of a growing body of literature that assesses the outcomes associated with women's studies courses and programs, the author asserts the parallel nature of these two types of curricular innovations. Studies focusing on the impact of women's studies courses conclude that the outcomes for students were positive. For example, women who enrolled in women's studies courses were more likely to consider themselves feminists. They were also more likely to have more positive attitudes towards men, and have significant positive changes in self-esteem scores. Further, research studies on the impact of women's studies programs indicate that they contribute significantly and positively to their campuses.

===

Frederick D. Patterson Research Institute. 1997. *The African American education data book.* Higher and Adult Education, vol. 1. Virginia: The College Fund/United Negro College Fund.

This is a comprehensive collection of data on the history and current state of African Americans in U. S. higher education. Information is provided on student and staff participation in higher education, graduation rates, financial aid, degrees awarded, institutional selection, post- graduation jobs, and test performance. Some of the data sources include: the U. S. Census Bureau, the Integrated Postsecondary Education Data System, the National Postsecondary Student Aid Study, the Beginning Postsecondary Student Survey, the Baccalaureate and Beyond survey, and the College Board. While the study is directed to African Americans, it provides valuable comparative information for the population at large and other ethnic groups.

━━

Friedlander, J., and P. MacDougall. 1992. Achieving student success through student involvement. *Community College Review* 20 (1): 20–28.
In this study, 1,765 students completed the Community College Student Experience Questionnaire in 1989. Among the findings of the research is that students at different levels of involvement show significant differences in perceptions of their own progress. A variety of programs designed to increase student involvement have been instituted at Santa Barbara City College, including a faculty advising project and on-campus jobs involving teaching.

━━

Friedman, D. L. 1990. Minorities in engineering school: A data base for retention efforts. *National Action Council for Minorities in Engineering (NACME) Research Letter* 1 (1). ERIC, ED 326593.
The National Action Council for Minorities in Engineering conducted a national survey of underrepresented students in engineering to find a program that would increase the number of graduates from such groups in engineering. The survey revealed the need for financial assistance, support programs, early exposure of youth to engineers, faculty who are sensitive to diverse students, and the need for the reduction of ethnic conflict in the campus environment.

━━

Frierson, H., B. Hargrove, and N. Lewis. 1994. Black summer research students' perceptions related to research mentor's race and gender. *Journal of College Student Development* 35:475–480.
This study examined the perceptions and attitudes of African American students who were in the "prementoring" stage of a faculty mentor relationship. The study revealed African American students with African American or female mentors had a more positive perception and attitude toward research than their peers with white male mentors.

━━

Fuertes, J. N., M. Cothran, and W. E. Sedlacek. 1991. A model for increasing Hispanic student involvement on U. S. campuses. *College Student Affairs Journal* 11 (2): 11–15.
The model presented in this report is based on research that shows that some Latino/as at predominantly white universities are active and find themselves in the mainstream of campus life, while others have more difficulty integrating themselves into college. With the increasing number of Latino/as attending college, it has become more important to encourage involvement on campus. This model proposes methods to reduce the perceived size of the campus for Latino/a students and to increase their sense of belonging. The goals of the model are increased retention and development of Latino/a students. The model increases student participation in a campus-wide Latino/a group, in Latino/a pre-professional societies, enrollment in a student development course, and participation in a mentoring program.

━━

Fuertes, J. N., and W. E. Sedlacek. 1995. Using noncognitive variables to predict the grades and retention of Hispanic students. *College Student Affairs Journal* 14 (2): 30–36.

The authors report the results of a ten-year longitudinal study of 156 Latino/a college students. A noncognitive survey of the students' ability to realize and understand racism, both institutional and interpersonal, was a predictor of the students' grades in the first three semesters of college, although the variables did not predict overall long-term retention.

===

Fuertes, J. N., W. E. Sedlacek, and W. M. Liu. 1994. Using the SAT and noncognitive variables to predict the grades and retention of Asian American university students. *Measurement and Evaluation in Counseling and Development* 27 (2): 74–84.

The authors examined the value of both SAT scores and measures of noncognitive variables as predictors of GPA and retention of 431 Asian American students. Both SAT and noncognitive variables were significant predictors.

===

Fukuyama, M. A., and N. C. Coleman. 1992. A model for bicultural assertion training with Asian-Pacific American college students: A pilot study. *Journal for Specialists in Group Work* 17 (4): 210–217.

Two groups of Asian-Pacific American students received different types of treatment in a study of the impact of bicultural assertiveness training on college students. One group participated in a five-week assertiveness training workshop, the other participated in an afternoon program. All participants took the College Self-Expression Scale (CSES) before and after the group experience. The students in the five-week workshop group increased the mean score on the CSES from 109.5 to 122.2 while the group receiving only the afternoon program scored 114.6 and 116.2 on the CSES test-retest. Significance was not computed because the groups numbered only eight and five. The bicultural group experience seems to have had a positive impact on the assertiveness of the participants.

===

Fullilove, R. E., and P. U. Treisman. 1990. Mathematics achievement among African American undergraduates at the University of California, Berkeley: An evaluation of the mathematics workshop program. *Journal of Negro Education* 59:463–478.

An evaluation of the Mathematics Workshop Program (MWP) developed by Uri Treisman is discussed in this work. The MWP is an honors program at University of California, Berkeley enrolling 80 percent African American and Latino/a participants. The objective of the evaluation was to assess the degree to which the MWP impacted the mathematics performance and persistence of students, as measured by a comparison of final Mathematics 1A grades earned by MWP and non-MWP students. When the proportion of students earning grades of B minus or better are compared by year and by membership in MWP, dramatic, statistically significant group differences emerge. MWP students were two to three times more likely to earn grades at this level of achievement than non-MWP students. The data clearly suggest that MWP has succeeded in achieving its primary objectives of promoting high levels of academic performance among African American and Latino/a mathematics students. The MWP has demonstrated a capacity to succeed in promoting high levels of academic achievement of minority students at a competitive, top-ranked university. The model has also proven to be highly adaptable to other institutions.

Gainen, J. 1995. Barriers to success in quantitative gatekeeper courses. In *Fostering student success in quantitative gateway courses*, edited by J. Gainen and E. W. Willemsen. New Directions for Teaching and Learning, no. 61. San Francisco: Jossey-Bass.
This article reviews the literature on student performance in mathematics. College preparation, peer culture, the classroom climate, and the competitive, impersonal culture of many mathematics courses are partial causes for students not performing well in math and science courses. For the limited number of students of color who receive pre-college mathematics instruction, the instruction tends to be limited and taught by poorly trained teachers. For the truly academically prepared, the lack of academic achievement can be traced to negative peer culture as described in Holland and Eisenhart's study of women who quickly forsook their academics to focus on being attractive. The workshops and studies of Treisman, Bonsangue and Drew, and Krupnicks are reviewed as well.

===

García, T., S. L. Yu, and B. Coppola. 1993. Women and minorities in science: Motivational and cognitive correlates of achievement. Paper presented at the annual meeting of the American Educational Research Association, April, at Atlanta, GA. ERIC, ED 359235.
This paper discusses the psychological factors in science achievement found in 557 college organic chemistry students. Correlations were found between prior achievement and motivation for African Americans, prior learning strategies and achievement for Asian American and white students, prior achievement and motivation for males, and prior learning strategies and achievement for females.

===

Garmon, M. A. 1996. Missed messages: How prospective teachers' racial attitudes mediate what they learn from a course on diversity. Ph.D. dissertation, Michigan State University. Abstract in *Dissertation Abstracts International* 57 (09): 3896A.
This dissertation studied the impact of a course in multicultural education on the racial attitudes and beliefs of a group of 200 prospective teachers. It also sought to determine if there were significant differences between those students whose racial attitudes and beliefs were initially favorable and those whose racial attitudes and beliefs were initially unfavorable. The study was based on a pre- and post-test administration of a survey of racial attitudes and a teaching/learning questionnaire. Some of the participants were also interviewed regularly throughout the semester. The significant finding of the study was that students' initial racial attitudes and beliefs played a major role in mediating the impact of the course. Students who began the course with more positive and favorable racial beliefs were more likely to change in the direction intended based on the course content than students who began the course with less positive racial attitudes and beliefs.

===

Geasler, M. J., J. M. Croteau, C. J. Heineman, and C. J. Edlund. 1995. A qualitative study of students' expression of change after attending panel presentations by lesbian, gay, and bisexual speakers. *Journal of College Student Development* 36:483–492.
Using over 400 pages of textual data from 260 students in five human sexuality and family relationships classes, the authors evaluated the effects of a regularly scheduled

panel discussion by lesbians and gays. Most speakers were fellow students while others were former students of the university. An immediate reaction to the panel was collected from students after the presentation, including a description of the events in the presentation most significant to them and a response to the question, "In what ways has this presentation caused changes in your attitudes or feelings about homosexuality?" A second assignment, "Please use the space below to fully describe your reactions to the panel," was distributed for completion by the next class meeting. Students' changes as a result of the panel were almost exclusively positive. Among the statements of change, the themes of dispelling stereotypes, commonality, empathy with struggle, and self-reflection dominated. The authors found that students who were initially positive toward lesbians and gays deepened their positive attitudes. The process of writing feelings after the presentation may also solidify learning.

===

Gilbert, W. S. 1996. Bridging the gap between high school and college: A successful program that promotes academic success for Hopi and Navajo students. Paper presented at the Retention in Education for Today's American Indian Nations conference, April, at Tucson, AZ. ERIC, ED 398039.

Gilbert reports on a large scale cooperative program between Northern Arizona University and students in seven high schools on or near Navajo and Hopi reservations. An academic year program for 9,635 students in grades seven through twelve included retention, career development, and computer-assisted instruction components. A summer program at Northern Arizona included instruction in English, math, and career development for 498 ninth through eleventh graders, exposing them to collegiate life.

===

Gilliard, M. D. 1996. Racial climate and institutional support factors affecting success in predominantly white institutions: An examination of African-American and white student experiences. Ph.D. dissertation, University of Michigan. Abstract in *Dissertation Abstracts International* 57 (04): 1515A.

This study examined the impact of campus racial climate on the success of African American and white students at six predominantly white Midwestern colleges and universities. The study specifically examined the effects of structural characteristics of the institution, general experiences common to students, race related experiences of African American students, general and racially focused support services on academic achievement, educational aspirations, and sense of belonging. The study used the responses of 896 African American and 1211 white undergraduate students to the Midwest Colleges Study administered in 1990 and 1991. The study concludes that an institutional racial climate that supports and affirms people from racially and ethnically diverse backgrounds is important for the success of all students. The study also suggests a need for administrators to play a lead role in promoting racial and ethnic diversity.

===

Gilman, C. W. 1994. Listen to our voices: Student experiences of cultural diversity at the University of Virginia. Ph.D. dissertation, University of Virginia. Abstract in *Dissertation Abstracts International* 55 (05): 1198A.

This was a qualitative study to examine students' experiences with culturally diverse others during their first three years as undergraduates at the University of Virginia.

The study consisted of hour-long interviews with twelve students at the end of their third year of college. The twelve students included four each of African American, Asian American, and white students. Within each racial group, two students were male and two female. The interviews were designed to gather responses to three questions: "In what ways do students at the University of Virginia experience cultural diversity? How have they been affected or influenced by those experiences? How might a more open and comfortable environment of campus diversity be fostered?" Responses were grouped by race and analyzed. The data identify several points: strong racial stereotypes continue among students; racial isolation and clustering of students continue to exist; students feel the university is encouraging and supporting an open environment and feel that many of the negative experiences are the result of individual student actions and interactions.

==

Gobbo, K., and J. A. Bolaski. 1997. Understanding the concerns of college students with learning disabilities and attention deficit disorders. *Student Affairs Journa–Online* [online]. Available at http://www.sajo.org.

This online article reviews the literature on students with learning disabilities and attention deficit disorders. Gobbo and Bolaski also provide links to several relevant World Wide Web sites for more information.

==

Gold, J., S. Burrell, C. Haynes, and D. Nardecchia. 1990. *Student adaptation to college as a predictor of academic success: An exploratory study of black undergraduate education students.* ERIC, ED 331946.

This article reports on a study aimed at investigating the relationship between the perceptions of undergraduate African American students of their adjustment to a predominantly white university and levels of academic success. The study included a sample of twenty-three African American females and six African American male freshman education students at a mid-sized, Midwestern university. Their responses to the Student Adaptation to College Questionnaire (SACQ) were correlated with their grade point average (GPA) using multiple regression analysis. The findings revealed a significant correlation between total SACQ scores and GPA. Scores on the academic adjustment subscale were significant predictors of academic success for women. Scores on the personal-emotional subscale were significant predictors of academic success for men. Based on these findings, the author recommends positive intervention for women may include personal counseling, tutoring, skill building, time management, and term paper writing.

==

Gossett, B. J., M. J. Cuyjet, and I. Cockriel. 1996. African Americans' and non-African Americans' sense of mattering and marginality at public, predominantly white institutions. *Equity and Excellence in Education* 29 (3): 37–42.

This study compared opinions of African American and non-African American undergraduate students regarding their sense of mattering. One thousand one-hundred eighty participants from four predominantly white institutions in the Midwest participated in the study. The authors found considerable differences between the perception of African American students and their non-African American peers on issues of mattering and marginality. They also found that many policies at predominantly white institutions were not sensitive to the African American student. Practical ways of enhancing the learning of all students were discussed.

==

Grant, C. A., and W. G. Secada. 1990. Preparing teachers for diversity. In *Handbook of research in teacher education*, edited by W. R. Houston. New York: Macmillan. ERIC, ED 318735.

This chapter presents a review of the literature that focuses on assessing the impact of diversity initiatives on pre-service teachers. In particular, the authors present the small number of studies that provide empirical validation of claims about the effectiveness of specific diversity efforts. They discovered sixteen studies published between 1973 and 1988 that assessed the effect of multicultural education on pre-service teachers. Thirteen of these studies focused exclusively on individual programs. Six of the studies were pre-test/post-test design; the others used post-test only. The majority used self-report attitude surveys to assess program effectiveness. Most of the instruments were designed by the researchers. In terms of overall findings, only one study reported clearly positive results. The remaining studies reported mixed results; however, all of the researchers cited conclude that multicultural pre-service education is important. A key conclusion drawn by the researchers is that the most effective strategies involve the intense exposure to diversity issues. Further, the more time spent learning the content, the more varied the presentation, and the more that coursework covers these issues, the more likely learning will be successful.

==

Gray, M. J., G. Vernez, and E. Rolph. 1996. Student access and the "new" immigrants: Assessing their impact on institutions. *Change* 28 (5): 41–47.

This report summarizes two research studies conducted by the authors for the Rand Corporation. The research analyzed both immigrant students and institutions, focusing on fourteen colleges and universities in areas of the country that are receiving large numbers of immigrants. Regarding access, the researchers discovered that immigrant students are more likely to be enrolled in a college preparatory program in high school (almost 50 percent of immigrant high school students were enrolled in an academic track compared to just over 40 percent of native-born high school students). Almost three-fourths of immigrant students plan to attend college compared to two-thirds of native-born students. Sixty-eight percent of immigrant high school graduates actually enroll in college, compared to sixty percent of native-born graduates. The institutional component of the study reveals that: immigrants are not generally identified as a special population on college campuses; faculty and administrators believe that immigrant students do better than they do; language skills are the greatest barrier to immigrant students; there is institutional opposition to the creation of special programs for immigrant students; and the complexity of federal and state policies on immigrant students leads to uneven and possibly unfair implementation. The authors conclude that institutions and society at large must become more aware of the issues of immigrant students and determine how best to respond to this growing population.

==

Green, S., P. Dixon, and V. Gold-Neil. 1993. The effects of a gay/lesbian panel discussion on college student attitudes toward gay men, lesbians, and persons with AIDS (PWAs). *Journal of Sex Education and Therapy* 19 (1): 47–63.

This study assessed the effectiveness of a lesbian and gay panel presentation in a human sexuality class of fifty-two women and twenty-seven men. Seniors composed 42 percent of the class and people of color composed 9 percent. The panel used three lesbians and two gay males from the local community, only one of whom was a college student. The presentation included personal stories by each panel member, a question and answer period, and informal interaction with the class to provide one-on-one contact between panel members and students. A pre-test, post-test comparison of scores found women's attitudes were significantly less negative on the post-test and men's attitudes were not significantly changed. On the post-test, androgynous males had the most negative attitudes while feminine women scored the lowest on negativity. Both those acquainted with and not acquainted with gays and lesbians showed significant increases in positive attitudes after the panel. Many other correlations with student group characteristics are also reported.

Grimes, S. 1995. Targetory academic programs to student diversity utilizing styles and learning-study strategies. *Journal of College Student Development* 36:422–430.
This article reports on a study that analyzes learning style and learning-study strategies for varied risk levels, for selected risk groups, and by specific student characteristics. Data were collected from 394 students in an open community college with approximately 8,000 students and a 15 percent minority enrollment. The group included 138 high-risk students, 188 students representing the entering population, and sixty-eight low-risk students. Significant differences were found in learning style by group, gender, and age. It revealed that African American students did not differ from non-minority students in learning styles or study strategies despite lower academic preparation. The research suggests that many at-risk students with a history of lower academic performance may be perpetuating their risk by their choice of learning-study strategies. The differences in learning style and learning-study strategies suggest further research is needed as to the utilization of similar diagnostic models.

Guarasci, R., and G. H. Cornwell, eds. 1997. *Democratic education in an age of difference: Redefining citizenship in higher education.* San Francisco: Jossey-Bass.
This book describes some of the programmatic and curricular innovations designed to address issues of citizenship and multicultural fluency on a number of college campuses. Programs in residential learning communities, service learning, intergroup relations, and women's studies are described. The book highlights some of the important issues about how the design of programs influences the outcomes for students. The authors also highlight the positive impact of many of these programs on student learning and attitudes, such as an increased capacity to deal with differences, to cross boundaries, and to engage in discussion on difficult issues.

Guarasci, R. 1997. Community-based learning and intercultural citizenship. In *Democratic education in an age of difference: Redefining citizenship in higher education,* edited by R. Guarasci and G. H. Cornwell. San Francisco: Jossey-Bass.
Guarasci describes an effective service-learning program that works to develop student awareness of the responsibilities of citizenship in a diverse society. The program links academic course work, student volunteer activities, and community based learning in which the external community plays a role in determining the content of the experi-

ence, not just as the recipient of student voluntary service. The effectiveness of the program is measured through analysis of student reflective essays on their experiences. Results show an increase of student awareness of the values of diversity and increasing sophistication in working with communities.

===

Guon, D. G. 1988. Minority access and retention: An evaluation of a multi-university peer counseling program. Paper presented at a meeting of the Midwestern Psychological Association, at Chicago, IL.

At three universities, talented minority upperclassmen were trained as peer counselors for at-risk minority students. Peer counselors met regularly with their counselees to provide academic tutoring, social support, and positive social role modeling. Data on first and second term GPA, high school GPA, and standardized test scores were collected for 112 participating at-risk minority students, 111 non-minority students not in the program, and 99 at-risk minority students not in the program. Multiple regression analysis revealed that program membership, followed by first term GPA, were the strongest predictors of year-end enrollment status. Eighty two percent of the program students were retained as compared to 74 percent of the non-program students.

===

Harrington, H. L., and R. S. Hathaway. 1995. Illuminating beliefs about diversity. *Journal of Teacher Education* 46 (4): 275–284.

The article investigates the effectiveness of computer conferencing as a way to identify students' beliefs about diversity, multiculturalism, and multicultural education.

===

Harwarth, I., M. Maline, E. DeBra. 1997. *Women's colleges in the United States: History, issues, and challenges.* Washington, DC: National Institute on Postsecondary Education, Libraries, and Lifelong Learning, U.S. Department of Education.

This monograph is a compilation of national statistics, history, and policy issues related to the impact and contribution of women's colleges in the United States. The report summarizes research demonstrating the impact of women's colleges on degree attainment, satisfaction, leadership, and other outcomes.

===

Hasslen, R. C. 1993. The effects of teaching strategies in multicultural education on monocultural students' perceptions. Ph.D. dissertation, University of Minnesota. Abstract in *Dissertation Abstracts International* 55 (01): 4668A.

This dissertation examined the effects of teaching strategies on white students in a multicultural education course. The research involved administering three pre- and post-treatment attitude and opinion surveys to students in three sections of a multicultural education course. In addition to the surveys, data from demographic surveys, journals, and student memos were analyzed. The author concludes: a single course in multicultural education has a definite impact on altering student perceptions of cultural diversity; different teaching strategies have different impacts on the perceptions of racism and equity issues; pairing white students with students of color leads to the lessening of myths and a decline in the fear of difference; and demographic differences in students do not limit the effectiveness of the course.

===

Hawley, W. D., and A. W. Jackson, eds. 1995. *Toward a common destiny: Improving race and ethnic relations in America.* San Francisco: Jossey-Bass.

This book includes a series of chapters summarizing the available studies on the implications for schools of the research on race relations in America. These studies, while almost entirely focusing in K-12 levels of education, show strong support for the role of curricular content, cooperative learning, and ethnic identity development on intergroup relations and attitude change. The research also supports four basic conditions for positive intergroup contact: equal status; common goals; institutional support; and interaction as individuals.

——

Holland, J. 1993. Relationship between African American doctoral students and their major advisors. Paper presented at the annual meeting of the American Educational Research Association, April, at Atlanta, GA.

This study examined the relationship between students and major advisors and identified those factors potentially guiding and motivating African American doctoral students to pursue careers in higher education. The findings clearly indicate African American doctoral students experience various relationships and involvements with their faculty advisors, and of these relationships, the student-advisor was the most nonsatisfying. Of the five relationships studied, academic mentoring, career mentoring, and quasi-apprenticeship had the most significant impact on the students seeking careers in higher education.

——

Hood, D. 1990. A look at retention of Afro-American male students at a predominantly white institution. Paper presented at the annual meeting of the American Educational Research Association, April, at Boston, MA.

The purpose of this paper is to examine programmatic support services and their impact on African American males at a large, predominantly white public university. It reports the success of a peer-assisted learning project with three cohorts of African American males enrolled in programs in Northern Illinois University Education Services and Programs office. It also suggests areas for future research.

——

Hood, S., and L. Parker. 1994. Minority students informing the faculty: Implications for racial diversity and the future of teacher education. *Journal of Teacher Education* 45 (3): 164–171.

Hood and Parker report on interviews with minority teacher education students discussing the impact the lack of diversity has on their abilities to teach.

——

Howard-Vital, M. R., and R. Morgan. 1993. *African American women and mentoring.* ERIC, ED 360425.

This study explores the mentoring experiences of African American women in higher education and its potential for improving their status. A pilot study was designed using Blackwell's ten functions of a mentor to examine the subjects' perception of mentoring. The respondents' most perceived function of a mentor was to build self-confidence, increase self-esteem, and strengthen motivation. The second most frequently identified function was "socializing protégés regarding role requirements, expectations, and organizational imperatives." The findings of this study reinforced Blackwell's two functions of a mentor but did not identify any gender or race specific functions.

Hummel, M. L. 1997. Eliminating the achievement gap: The 21st Century Program. *About Campus* 1 (6): 28–29.

This article summarizes a support program at the University of Michigan intended to increase the retention rates of students in general, and African American students in particular. The program is based on the work of Claude Steele who argues that support services directed specifically at students of color are based on racial stereotypes and undermine academic performance. Approximately 600 first-year students, one-third students of color, are placed in a seminar entitled "The College Student." The author outlines the seminar, summarizes its components, and highlights some of its results. On average, program participants at every preparatory level have achieved higher than students not in the program. Specifically, the retention rate of African American students was approximately 92 percent compared to the 70 percent graduation rate for African Americans in the university at large.

Hummel, M., and C. Steele. 1996. The learning community: A program to address issues of academic achievement and retention. *Journal of Intergroup Relations* 23 (2): 28–33.

The authors describe the 21st Century Program at the University of Michigan, a program developed in 1991 to enhance the academic and social experience and student success at a large state university. The program was modeled on the work of Claude Steele, who identified pressures and stereotypes leading to less successful performance by students of color. Treisman's work with the Math Workshop was influential as well. The program sought to create an "undergraduate community focused on academics" with a supportive environment, "to enhance student success," "to develop an interest in learning," and to make the university "a more personal experience." The program was not specifically directed to students of color, only 35 percent of 265 participants were students of color. Participants were assigned to a living area and many registered in at least one class together. Other program activities included: subject mastery workshops in which collaborative learning was practiced with an underlying belief in student achievement; a seminar and small group discussions; and other community building activities. Student achievement by program participants was higher than for non-participants and the graduation rate for the first class of African American students in the program was 92 percent. Controlling for race and preparation level as measured by SAT or ACT scores, first semester grades of program participants were higher than those of non-participants. For students in the top two-thirds of the sample, there was no difference in grades of white and non-white students. Although this was only a first year program, the differential success of participants continued through the sophomore year. After the sophomore year the difference did not continue, possibly because the average grade of non-participants rose as students dropped out of the university or the grades of participants fell as they took more difficult classes. The program has grown and faces the challenges of increased numbers of participants.

Hune, S. 1997. Higher education as gendered space: Asian American women and everyday inequities. In *Everyday sexism in the third millennium,* edited by C. Rambo Ronai, B. A. Zsembik, and J. R. Feagin. New York: Routledge.

Hune's essay examines the current status of Asian American women in American higher education and suggests reasons for that situation. She explores participation in and opportunities for Asian American women at all levels, from undergraduate through faculty member. Although many barriers to participation and success in higher education have been removed, Hune identifies continuing obstacles for Asian American women and other minority group members. Asian American women are restrained as women, as minority group members, and especially by their membership in what has historically been considered the "model minority." At the doctorate and faculty level, although progress is being made, Asian American women are still excluded by practices and processes that seem to maintain power where it currently resides. Hune calls for the opening of access as well as the creation of spaces and places that are empowering for Asian American women and others.

Hune, S., and K. S. Chan. 1997. *Special focus: Asian Pacific American demographic and educational trends. Fifteenth annual status report.* Washington, DC: American Council on Education.

This special report focuses on Asian Pacific Americans. The summary suggests that the civil rights history of Asian Americans can serve as a basis for discussing educational equity, climate, educational, and economic issues. The analysis illuminates the inadequacy of using population demographics as a sufficient indicator of educational equity and describes the absence of attention to issues of Asian Americans in terms of climate and education. The demographic section provides a current picture of the diversity of the Asian American population as well as the diversity of the educational and economic experiences of specific populations.

Hunt, P., J. Schmidt, S. Hunt, V. Boyd, and T. Magoon. 1994. The value of the undergraduate experience to African American students. *Journal of College Student Development* 35:282–288.

This longitudinal study of 134 African Americans examines the perceptions of undergraduate experiences, as well as adaptation to life beyond the campus ten years after entering college. This article compares the perceptions, differences, and similarities of African Americans who earned a baccalaureate degree and those who did not. Of the 134 responding to the survey (out of 176 possible participants), 66 percent had completed at least the baccalaureate degree. The study suggests that those who earned an undergraduate degree performed significantly better academically than those who left college before graduating. The non-graduates also perceived the campus community as uncomfortable, but found once leaving the academic environment, their self confidence increased. There was no significant difference between the two groups in relation to intimacy and interpersonal relationships; however, there was a significant difference in decision making with the non-graduates expressing difficulty. There were no significant differences in the respondents' perceptions of intellectual development after college, but there were significant differences between their scores on the quantitative part of the SAT. Sixty-nine of the non-graduates reported having plans to complete their undergraduate degree with a more realistic view of their career plans and goals.

Hurtado, S. 1992. The campus racial climate: Contexts of conflict. *Journal of Higher Education* 63:539–569.

This study draws upon several data sources to focus on the experiences of a particular student cohort that attended predominantly white colleges from 1985 to 1989, a period

when racial incidents occurred on many campuses. Findings show that no single element produces racial tension on college campuses, but that a configuration of external
influences, structural characteristics of institutions and group relations, and institutionalized ideologies shape the campus climate.

———. 1994a. Graduate school racial climates and academic self-concept among minor-
    ity graduate students in the 1970s. *American Journal of Education* 102:330–351.
Longitudinal data on African Americans and Latino/a students attending graduate
school since the 1970s are used to test a model reflecting the influence of parental
socioeconomic status, gender, pre-college assessments, and the graduate school's racial
climate on academic self-concept change as students move into adulthood. Minority
women consistently lag behind men in perceptions of their academic self-concept.
Higher academic self-concept was reported in graduate racial climates characterized
by low trust and interaction among groups.

———. 1994b. The institutional climate for talented Latino students. *Research in Higher
    Education* 35:21–41.
The experience of high-achieving Latino/a students at various types of institutions was
the subject of this study. Semifinalists in the National Latino/a Scholar Awards program were studied using SAT and Student Descriptive Questionnaire (administered in
conjunction with the SAT) data, a mailed survey (the National Survey of Latino/a
Students), institutional data from the Integrated Postsecondary Education Data
Systems (IPEDS), and other institutional data files. Altogether, 859 sophomores and
juniors attending 224 colleges and universities were analyzed in the sample.
Institutional characteristics which entered the regression analysis as associated with a
hostile climate for Latino/a students included a large campus, students who don't know
about Latino/a culture, and location in a small town. High Latino/a enrollment, an
open and inclusive administration, and caring faculty were all associated with a positive climate. The results are of interest to those wishing to construct more positive environments for all students.

———. 1996. How diversity affects teaching and learning: A climate of inclusion has a
    positive effect on learning outcomes. *Educational Record* 66 (4): 27–29.
The author discusses the impact of diversity in higher education on teaching and learning. The growth of a diverse student population leads to increased research on learning styles, emphasis on quantitative and scientific literacy, and new research on student
issues in learning.

Hurtado, S., and D. F. Carter. 1994. Latino students' sense of belonging in the college
    community: Rethinking the concept of integration on campus. Paper presented at
    the annual meeting of the American Educational Research Association, April, at
    New Orleans, LA.
In this study, 272 high-achieving Latino/a students enrolled in 127 colleges and universities in 1990 were surveyed to examine their changes in attitudes, activities, and
experiences. The study examined the influence of seven critical factors, namely: sense
of belonging on campus, academic self-concept, cognitive mapping, managing
resources, separation from family, experiencing discrimination or exclusion, and per-

ceptions of racial and ethnic tensions on campus. The study shows that students belonging to religious organizations and members of Greek organizations had a stronger sense of belonging on campus than those who did not belong to these organizations. Similarly, members of religious clubs, social/community groups, and student government had a stronger sense of belonging than non-participants. Members of ethnic groups, however, did not have a stronger sense of belonging than those not involved in ethnic groups. The study also found that selectivity of the college had a negative effect on transition to college, that an easier transition to college had a negative effect on perceptions of a hostile campus climate, and that perceptions of a hostile climate had a negative impact on sense of belonging. Student background was related to college selectivity but unrelated to other variables.

===

———. Forthcoming. College transition, campus racial climate perceptions, and sense of belonging among Latino college students. *Sociology of Education.*

A national study of Latino/a students reveals that perceptions of racial/ethnic tensions in the second year of college have a negative effect on the students' sense of belonging within the overall college community in the third year of college.

===

Hurtado, S., D. F. Carter, and S. Sharp. 1995. Social interaction on campus: Differences among self-perceived ability groups. Paper presented at the annual meeting of the Association for Institutional Research, March, at Boston, MA. ERIC, ED 387014.

This paper discusses the possible connections between perceived academic level, social involvement, and interaction across race in everyday campus situations. The sample consisted of 4,138 Asian American, African American, white, and Latino/a students from 291 four-year colleges and universities. High ability students in honors classes are more likely to be enrolled in difficult courses than students who perceived themselves as low or medium ability students. These same high ability students, according to the authors, also are more likely to eat, socialize, date, and develop informal relationships with students from different ethnic backgrounds. Middle ability students tended to work off-campus and participate in Greek life off-campus and low ability students tended to play sports.

===

Hurtado, S., D. F. Carter, and A. Spuler. 1996. Latino student transition to college: Assessing difficulties and factors in successful college adjustment. *Research in Higher Education* 37: 135–157.

The author used a national longitudinal survey of National Merit semifinalists to look at factors which relate to the college adjustment of gifted Latino/a students. Student background accounted for the lowest component of the measures of adjustment. In contrast, campus climate, perceptions about a student-centered focus to the institution, experiences of discrimination, and faculty interaction were all related to adjustment. Resident advisors, counselors, and upper class students played a positive, supportive role.

===

Hurtado, S., E. L. Dey, and J. G. Treviño. 1994. Exclusion or self-segregation?: Interaction across racial/ethnic groups on college campuses. Paper presented at

the annual meeting of the American Educational Research Association, April, at New Orleans, LA.
Using the 1987 freshman class and follow-up data from 1991, this study investigates patterns of interracial groups on campuses across the country as a function of demographic makeup of the campus, campus climate, institutional characteristics, and student characteristics. Results demonstrate the myth of self-segregation as it applies to students of color. White students, however, clearly had even fewer interactions across groups. The results suggest that involvement, climate, and diversity of the student body, among other factors, were all related to the level of intergroup interactions.

Hurtado, S., J. F. Milem, W. R. Allen, and A. R. Clayton-Pedersen. 1996. *Improving the climate for racial/ethnic diversity in higher education.* Report to the Common Destiny Alliance. College Park, MD.
This report summarizes the literature on diversity and its impact on students—quite similar to our present study—and offers a series of recommendations for improving institutional practices. The authors also describe several exemplary programs from colleges and universities around the country. An excellent bibliography is included.

Hyun, M. 1996. Commitment to change: How college impacts changes in students' commitment to racial understanding. Ph.D. dissertation, University of California, Los Angeles. Abstract in *Dissertation Abstracts International* 57 (05): 1978A.
This dissertation uses the Cooperative Institutional Research Project freshman survey of 1985 and the 1989 senior follow-up to examine whether colleges and universities have an impact on students' commitment to promote racial understanding. The study also looks for any differences in the impact on white and African American students. The study explores the relationship between students' commitment to racial tolerance and support for other forms of societal change. The study uses cross-tabulations and multiple regressions and attempts to control for the college and student factors. African American students' commitment to racial understanding increased at a greater rate than the commitment of white students, but there was a positive effect for both groups.

Increasing enrollment fees: Equity? or the allocation of opportunity? The effects of fees on student enrollment in the San Diego Community College District. 1993. San Diego, CA. Research and Planning Office, San Diego Community College District. ERIC, ED 362223.
This report documents the effects of the increase in community college fees on access for various groups. San Diego Community College District administered a questionnaire and found an enrollment decline of 8 percent when fees increased from $5 to $10 per unit. Student contact hours decreased weekly by 5 percent. Respondents to the survey (Asian American, 25 percent; African American, 9 percent; white, 7 percent) report that the higher fees would prohibit them from registering in the future. Also, the fee increase would prevent students aged forty-one or older from continuing their education. Students aged twenty-two to twenty-five were more likely to continue.

Institute for the Study of Social Change. 1995. Reprint. *The Diversity Project: Final report.* Berkeley, CA: University of California. Original edition, 1991.

This report represents a comprehensive ethnographic study of students on issues of diversity and multiculturalism. From 1989 through 1991, the researchers interviewed nearly 300 Berkeley students in 69 racially mixed and homogeneous groups. Troy Duster and his colleagues report that there is both a trend toward strong group affiliation and also significant student interest in experiencing greater levels of interaction across groups at Berkeley. The re-segmentation represents a voluntary resurgence in identification with ethnic clubs and patterns of affiliation. Meanwhile, a multicultural course requirement was found to lead students to greater appreciation of the complexity of cultural production in various cultures. In terms of student interactions, there is an eschewing of sensitivity sessions. Those students reporting positive interactions found them in cooperative learning situations created in classes and projects. The complexity of meeting is made more difficult because of naive racial attitudes by white students who see the issues as one-on-one meetings that allow them to experience the "other" without conflict, tension, bitterness, or hostility. The issue of racial politics is viewed very differently by whites and African Americans who make up polar ends of the spectrum, while Latino/as and Asian Americans fall between these two groups. A model of mutual enhancement is proposed as the goal for all students to experience diversity. A series of recommendations suggests faculty rhetorical responsibility in sensitive areas, student willingness to encounter each other in volunteer and other outside-the-classroom experiences, and a need for an on-going forum for the discussion of admissions and orientation issues especially during the first year.

═══

Jacobi, M. 1991. Mentoring and undergraduate academic success: A literature review. *Review of Higher Education* 61:505–533.

This article reviews pertinent literature on mentoring with an emphasis on the relationship between mentoring and academic success. It discusses the definition and empirical research of mentoring and the undergraduate student. It also describes institutions that have successful mentoring programs.

═══

Johnson, A. W., and J. A. Sullivan. 1995. Mentoring program practices and effectiveness. In *Mentoring: New strategies and challenges*, edited by M. W. Galbraith and N. H. Cohen. New Directions for Adult and Continuing Education, no. 66. San Francisco: Jossey-Bass.

The authors review the literature of mentoring programs and highlight several. Ten of the fifteen programs had quantitative evaluations. Almost thirty percent of all the findings suggest that mentoring programs have a positive effect on students. Only ten percent of the outcomes of mentoring programs were negative. Four out of ten programs found negative results. Two out of ten programs had positive and negative results. The last four programs had positive results with non-significant outcomes. Of these last four programs, academic support was offered with mentoring. It was found that one-to-one mentoring is helpful and meeting with students once a week is key to mentoring.

═══

Kardia, D. B. 1996. Diversity's closet: Student attitudes toward lesbians, gay men, and bisexual people on a multicultural campus. Ph.D. dissertation, University of Michigan. Abstract in *Dissertation Abstracts International* 57 (03): 1090A.

This is one of the first studies to look at how higher education impacts students' acceptance of sexual diversity. Using survey and interview data in a pre- and post-treatment model, this study examines change in student attitudes toward sexual diversity among 1041 students between 1990 and 1994. Five conclusions are drawn about the impact of college on student attitudes toward sexual diversity. First, college provides new opportunities for students to develop an understanding of sexual diversity. Second, contact with a bisexual, gay, or lesbian person is the primary method through which attitudes change. Third, indicators of moral, cognitive, and social development can be associated with a student's capacity for acceptance and openness to difference. Fourth, curricular and co-curricular consideration of sexual diversity creates opportunities for consideration of the issues and establishes norms of respect for that consideration. Finally, fraternities play a role in discouraging the acceptance of sexual diversity and religious groups play a role in reinforcing negative attitudes. These two factors work to create negative environments, despite progress in other areas on campus.

===

Kayabasi, M. 1988. Does the City College new world civilization course reduce provincialism? Paper presented at the annual meeting of the Northeastern Educational Research Association, May. ERIC, ED 350207.

This paper examines the extent to which students' interest in different cultures is affected by their participation in a world civilization course at the City College of the City University of New York. The researcher administered an initial questionnaire and a follow-up questionnaire to 184 first-year students. Thirteen of the participants, considered the control group, were not enrolled in the world civilization course. The questionnaire was designed to measure students' interests in, their perceptions of, and their actual knowledge about different cultures. The results of the study indicate no difference between the control group and those enrolled in the world civilization course in terms of student interest in diverse cultures. Both groups of students, those enrolled in the course and those in the control group, showed a significant increase in interest, self-perceived knowledge, and actual knowledge from the pre-test to the post-test. The author hypothesizes that the diverse nature of the student population at City College may contribute to students' experiences with cultural diversity and therefore their openness to the issue.

===

Keim, J., J. McWhirter, and B. Berstein. 1996. Academic success and university accommodation for learning disabilities: Is there a relationship? *Journal of College Student Development* 37:502–509.

The researchers looked at 125 students with learning disabilities and analyzed their use of several special services—academic advisement, computer support, tutoring, and test accommodation. Grade point average was used as the dependent variable. Class standing (freshman, sophomore, junior, senior) was also studied, but because of university cut-off scores for continuation, it was not considered in the analysis. Of the independent variables, only computer use was significantly correlated with cumulative GPA. Levels of advisement did not make a significant difference in cumulative GPA. Test accommodation and tutoring also did not show significant influence on cumulative GPA, although if the analysis was based on specific course grades, the outcome might be different. Overall, this study does not identify interventions that are significantly beneficial for learning disabled students.

Kenny, M. E., and S. Stryker. 1996. Social network characteristics and college adjustment among racially and ethnically diverse first-year students. *Journal of College
Student Development* 37:649–658.

Kenny and Stryker explore the social networks and support systems of a group of 218
first-year college students to determine which may have been related to self-reported
adjustment to college and to determine if the reported social networks differ across ethnicity. Participants in the survey were in a special support program for students of color
and white students who enrolled in a special advising program or special sections of
freshman English. Student social networks were assessed based on information about
the number and type of interactions they had with other students in a number of areas.
College adjustment was measured using the Student Adaptation to College
Questionnaire. There were significant differences in mean scores for network size and
satisfaction with college friend support, with non-white students reporting smaller
means in both cases. Multiple regression analysis was used to explore the relationships
of academic, personal, and social adjustment with the network variables. There were
differences in network variables entering the equations of adjustment based on ethnicity. A notable finding is that on-campus relationships have a differential importance for
white and non-white students—those relationships are highly related for white students
but not for others. Conversely, relationships with family were more highly related for
non-white students. This suggests the need for institutions to build links with families
of students of color as a means of supporting student success.

$$==$$

Kibble, J. F., M. A. Malmberg, and S. H. Ratwik. 1990. Capturing the experience of
Native American persisters: The exit interview vehicle. Paper presented at the
annual meeting of the American Educational Research Association, April, at
Boston, MA.

At Lake Superior University in 1989, interviews were held with nine American Indian
students who had graduated in either 1988 or 1989 and with ten American Indian students who had attended at least one term between 1983 and 1987 but had not completed their degrees. The data revealed that, in comparison to the student body as a
whole, the American Indian graduates were disproportionately represented in the
fields of business, engineering technology, legal assistant studies, and social sciences.
Although the graduates indicated that financial aid had not been a problem, tuition
waivers and scholarship support for books were cited as critical sources of support.
The graduates' perceptions of the campus experience varied widely according to
whether they were in a two- or four-year program. Family housing was cited as a crucial element, and the campus American Indian center was seen as the focus of support.
Five of the ten non-completers, in contrast to only one of the nine graduates, entered
the university as special status students. In addition to being less prepared academically, the non-completers had less clear goals, experienced more problems with the college
environment, had less satisfying relationships with advisers, and made less use of campus services. Many of the non-completers, however, had been on campus before most
of the American Indian services had been instituted.

$$==$$

Kleinsmith, L. J. 1993. Racial bias in science education. In *Multicultural teaching in the
university*, edited by D. Schoem, L. Frankel, X. Zúñiga, and E. Lewis. Westport,
CT: Praeger.

This chapter describes various reforms in science education and, in particular, the use of the computer at the college level to increase the representation of students of color in science. The approach described produced significant improvements in performance and satisfaction.

═══

Kraemer, B. A. 1997. The academic and social integration of Hispanic students into college. *Review of Higher Education* 20 (2): 193–179.

This study involved 217 Latino/a graduate students from a private, bilingual junior college in the Midwest. Three factors contributing to academic integration of Latino/a students were identified. Frequency of student participation in classroom discussion was the single indicator of formal faculty-student interaction. Second, study behavior was measured by frequency of use of the library. Finally, informal faculty-student interaction was measured by how often students met instructors outside of class to discuss academic topics. The study suggested the validity of academic and social integration for older, full-time Latino/a community college students. Both formal and informal faculty-student interactions have been shown to be strong predictors of integration into college and a strong influence on academic achievement and persistence.

═══

Laden, B. V., C. Sotello, and V. Turner. 1995. Viewing community college students through the lenses of gender and color. In *Gender and power in the community college*, edited by B. K. Townsen. New Directions for Community Colleges, no. 89. San Francisco: Jossey-Bass.

This article reviews the few studies of women of color in community colleges. The studies document the negative impact of domestic work and other family pressures on the academic progress of women. Special programs that support women of color financially and socially are needed. Assistance with transportation and child care is a major concern. Curricular reform, career information, and transfer information are also needed to assist women of color at community colleges.

═══

Lang, M. 1992. Barriers to blacks' educational achievement in higher education: A statistical and conceptual review. *Journal of Black Studies* 22:510–522.

This paper reviews the academic achievement of African Americans at secondary and postsecondary institutions. It provides a descriptive analysis of the trends, causes, and barriers to academic success, while offering an intervention mechanism to improve the success of African Americans in higher education.

═══

Lang, M., and C. A. Ford. 1992. *Strategies for retaining minority students in higher education*. Springfield, IL: Charles C. Thomas.

This book focuses on African American students. The first section presents a series of psycho-social portraits. The second section presents four case studies. The first, the Fenway Retention Consortium—a group of over twenty colleges in the Boston area organized in 1983—sought to increase postsecondary enrollment of Boston Public School graduates by 25 percent. The second examines cultural center administrators on predominantly white campuses. The third deals with an African American undergraduate student retention program. The final study describes a retention program in a medical school.

LeSure, G. E. 1993. Ethnic differences and the effects of racism on college adjustment. Paper presented at the annual meeting of the American Psychological Association, August, at Toronto, Canada. ERIC, ED 367936.

This study examines the relationship between demographics, academic and social adjustment, grade point average, racism experienced, and perceived racism at the five undergraduate Claremont Colleges in California. Respondents to the survey included 40 African Americans, 159 Asian Americans, 210 whites, 103 Latino/as, and 28 "others." The results of the study indicate that significantly more African Americans experienced racism than did their Latino/a or Asian American counterparts and that Latino/as and Asian Americans who did experience racism on campus showed poorer academic adjustment. The study also finds that all underrepresented students, regardless of race, showed lower social adjustment scores than their counterparts who did not experience racism.

=

Levin, J., and M. Levin. 1993. Methodological problems in research on academic retention programs for at risk minority college students. *Journal of College Student Development* 34:118–124.

This is an interesting and useful article addressing statistical and methodological issues of retention research. The authors review a number of articles in which they find methodological difficulties and point out how these difficulties compromise the quality of the reported results. Examples include questions of internal and external validity of the research question, the absence of meaningful data, the lack of meaningful comparison groups, issues with inappropriate randomization, non-comparable treatment, and bias by participants and investigators. While some readers might find such arguments to be a kind of intellectual "nit-picking," the issues identified in this article, and the solutions proposed by the author may help researchers produce studies that will be more useful and accepted in creating new programs and policies for the future.

=

Littleton, R., Jr. 1995. Perspectives on the black male college student's demise in the 1990s: Going, going ... gone? *Journal of African American Men* 1 (1): 75–82.

This report is a descriptive summary of factors that reflect the status of African American males in college. It offers summaries regarding the socio-economic status of the African American male, barriers to African American students entering college, problems facing the African American male while attending college, and efforts to retain the African American college student. It discusses in detail one successful model of a minority student summer program at the University of Florida which teaches students how to become successful in college. It also discusses the use of a multiracial sensitivity training session as a model for retaining African American male students in higher education.

=

Lomotey, K. 1990a. Culture and its artifacts in higher education: Their impact on the enrollment and retention of African American students. Paper presented at the annual meeting of the American Educational Research Association, April, at Boston, MA. ERIC, ED 319332.

Using interviews with faculty, staff, and students, this study examines the impact of institutional culture on the relatively high retention rate of African American students at Oberlin College. Lomotey reports the importance of vigilance in insuring the success

of African American students, the need for students to rely on one another, the importance of a critical mass of African American students on a predominantly white campus, and the need to hire, reward, and retain African American faculty and staff. Other
cultural aspects that contribute to retention include the historical image of the college,
its climate, sacred norms, and African American support institutions such as an
African American theme house, student organization, and African American Studies
department.

———. 1990b. The retention of African-American students: The effects of institutional
    arrangements in higher education. Paper presented at the Annual Meeting of the
    American Educational Research Association, April, at Boston, MA. ERIC, ED
    319333.
Lomotey uses Oberlin College as an example of an institution with a high retention rate
for African American students to study the impact of an African American theme
house, student organization, and a African American Studies department. In interviews with students, faculty, staff, and administrators, the author finds that the theme
house provided support and cultural enrichment, the student organization added political advantage, and the African American Studies department added status.

Lopez, G. E. 1993. The effect of group contact and curriculum on white, Asian
    American, and African American students' attitudes. Ph.D. dissertation,
    University of Michigan. Abstract in *Dissertation Abstracts International* 54 (07):
    3900B.
In a longitudinal survey of a sample of first-year students at the University of
Michigan, this study investigated the impact of intergroup contact and coursework
dealing with racial/ethnic issues on changes in student attitudes. While there were some
group differences, in general, coursework had the most significant positive impact on
increased support for educational equity. The results of intergroup contact were more
mixed with white students showing increased support for equity issues after contact.
This was not as true for African American students.

Luebke, B. F., and M. E. Reilly. 1995. *Women's studies graduates: The first generation.*
    New York: Teachers College Press. ERIC, ED 390312.
Using interview methodology, this study measured the impact of women's studies programs on student outcomes. It is particularly valuable in its description of the ways in
which students were studied for years following graduation and were asked to com-
ment on what they learned and gained from women's studies.

MacKay, K., and G. Kuh. 1994. A comparison of student effort and educational gains
    of Caucasian and African American students at predominantly white colleges and
    universities. *Journal of College Student Development* 35:217–223.
Using the College Student Experiences Questionnaire, the researchers explored the
amount of effort expended by white and African American students at predominantly
white colleges and universities as well as the contributions of those efforts to the learning and personal development of the students. The survey was distributed to more than
9,000 students at twelve institutions of different types. For analysis, a random sample
of responses from white students was selected so both groups were the same size.

Finally, the group was further limited by excluding older, married students. The final sample included 191 whites and 175 African Americans. Analysis included ANOVA to determine whether there were differences in levels of involvement and multiple regression to explore the relationships between effort and academic and social gain. Analysis identified no difference in quality of effort by ethnicity. The impact of quality of effort on gains was mixed with some factors influencing both groups and other factors influencing one or the other group. Peer interactions were positive and significant for both ethnic groups, supporting other research that collaborative work leads to both learning and personal development.

===

Maher, F. A., and M. K. T. Tetrault. 1994. *The feminist classroom.* New York: Basic Books.

This book represents the results of an in-depth study of feminist college professors on six college campuses using extensive interviews with faculty and students as well as observations. The book includes many reflections about what the outcomes of such work are and what short- and long-range impact might be obtained. The book also describes the complexity of engaging the issues of diversity in the classroom.

===

Maluso, D. 1992. Interventions to lessen racist prejudice and discrimination among college students. Ph.D. dissertation, University of Rhode Island. Abstract in *Dissertation Abstracts International* 53 (08): 4423B.

This dissertation studied the impact of exposure to either a high status minority group member (orientation leader) and/or a cultural diversity workshop on entering white students during a new student orientation program. Twelve weeks after orientation, students were given several tests to determine the impact of the various types of treatments. The outcome indicated that participation with the high status minority group member had a positive impact on later selection of a person of color in a photo choice task. Participation in the workshop did not make a significant difference on other responses.

===

Marchesani, J. J. 1994. Constellation prizes: Using science fiction for lesbian, gay, and bisexual issues in college classes. Paper presented at the Conference on College Composition and Communication, March, at Nashville, TN. ERIC, ED 370117.

Marchesani recounts his experience of teaching a freshman composition course with science fiction material that used narrative voices to present lesbian, gay, and bisexual characters as ordinary people. An abnormally high number of students (20 percent) quit the required class after seeing the texts and writing topics. The instructor received the lowest student course ratings for any course he had taught, 20 percent lower than another section of the course taught during the same term without these materials. The predominance of males in the class, who expected active and technical readings, may have contributed to the low ratings and high drop-out. The instructor/researcher determined that concentrating the entire syllabus on lesbian, gay, and bisexual material was counter-effective for integrating alternative sexualities as ordinary.

===

McCain-Reid, E. 1994. Seeds of change: A pilot study of senior pre-service teachers' responses to issues of diversity in one university course. Ph.D. dissertation, University of Toledo, OH. ERIC, ED 376227.

This study examines the impact on student learning of two models of instruction that were incorporated in a pre-service teacher education course. The two models were the Societal Curriculum/School Curriculum Model (SCSCM), which required students to keep an ongoing journal about diversity and to teach a lesson based on their observations and, the Multicultural Education Infusion Method (MEIM), which required students to write position papers comparing their philosophy of teaching to their ideas about diversity. Participants in this study were 16 white women, who were completing their last semester of a teacher education program at a small predominantly white university in Ohio. Respondents were surveyed at the beginning of the class to determine their attitudes about multicultural education and other issues of diversity. Despite previous exposure to diversity issues through coursework at the university, students generally demonstrated low levels of sophistication and experience regarding human diversity. As the course and the study progressed, students appeared to understand the concept of multicultural education but also had difficulty incorporating its themes into their assignments. Positive changes in attitudes did begin to occur, which suggests the usefulness of these approaches.

McEwen, M., and L. Roper. 1994. Interracial experiences, knowledge, and skills of master's degree students in graduate programs in student affairs. *Journal of College Student Development* 35:81–87.

The researchers report the results of a survey that simply sought to identify the perceptions of master's degree students in student affairs of their knowledge, experiences, and skills in areas of interracial experiences. The authors propose that competencies in cross-cultural areas are important, but that basic knowledge is a first step. Assessment of that knowledge can guide in the development of curriculum for college student development programs. Respondents, master's degree students in twenty-eight graduate programs, indicate that they have limited experience with people of color and need more knowledge about topics relating to students of color. The implications of the study for student affairs preparation programs are significant, exposing a need to develop curricular and experiential activities to increase knowledge and experience with issues of diversity. The authors also call for continuing research on the knowledge and experience level of new graduate students to determine the success of past activities.

McGrath, P., and F. Galaviz. 1996. The Puente Project. *About Campus* 1 (5): 27–28, 30.

This article summarizes the origin, content, and results of a project designed to address high dropout rates of Mexican American and Latino/a students in a community college setting. The model is described by outlining the specific actions required to build on the strengths of the students, including a combination of innovative teaching and counseling with community involvement. The success of the program has been duplicated at community colleges throughout California as well as transplanted to many high schools. The authors also describe some of the tangible outcomes of the project, primarily the high transferability and graduation rates of the Puente students. The concluding message is that programs targeting first-generation students need to consider them in the context of their family and culture and create a climate that appreciates differences among students.

Melaney, G., and M. Shively. 1995. Academic and social expectations and experiences
    of first-year students of color. *NASPA Journal* 33:3–18.

The researchers tested changes in students' social and academic expectations from the
start to finish of their first year, with the university as the intervention. Latino/a students significantly decreased their expectations of graduation and their belief that they
had made the right decision in attending the college. During the same period, the number of Asian American students who felt "they are a part of the university community
to a great extent" fell by half, yet Asian Americans significantly increased their perception that the university was making adequate efforts to fight racism. African
Americans significantly decreased their perception that the university was making an
adequate effort to make them feel comfortable and that they are a part of the university community. Meanwhile, the proportion of African American students engaging in
extracurricular activities increased by 24 percent. The only significant change for
white students was an increase in participation in extracurricular activities.

Merta, R. J., J. G. Ponterotto, and R. D. Brown. 1992. Comparing the effectiveness of
    two directive styles in the academic counseling of foreign students. *Journal of
    Counseling Psychology* 39 (2): 214–218.

Researchers attempted to determine whether authoritative or collaborative counseling
styles were differentially effective in working with foreign students in a university. Peer
counselors working with new international students were differently trained to be
authoritative or collaborative in their counseling styles. Independent raters rated the
counseling styles of the five counselors; the rated difference in their styles was statistically significant. A group of fifty Asian international students were counseled by the
five counselors using different styles. After single counseling sessions, the counselees
rated the counseling session. A follow-up interview and delayed rating took place about
ten days after the counseling session. Counselees were divided according to their acculturation level based on time in the United States and English proficiency. High acculturation students rated the authoritative counselors higher and low acculturation
students rated the collaborative counselors higher. This result seems counter to what
might be expected; students who were more acclimated to the cultural system wanted
to play a greater role in their counseling sessions. This research raises questions about
acculturation and counseling and advising styles for both international students and
U.S. minority students that need to be pursued.

Milem, J. F. 1994. College, students, and racial understanding. *Thought and Action* 9 (2):
    51–92.

Milem's study indicates that faculty attitudes and peer environments are related to
changes in student commitment to promoting racial understanding.

Minner, S., V. Bizardi, V. Arthur, J. Chischille, J. Holiday, R. Pyron, A. Rezzonico,
    and B. Yellowhair. 1995. Completing university degrees: Barriers for Native
    American. Paper presented at the meeting of the American Council on Rural
    Special Education, March, at Las Vegas, NV. ERIC, ED 381302.

This study reports on three informal surveys of American Indian community college
students. The first surveyed twenty-two students who dropped out of Northern
Arizona University. They identified family responsibilities, lack of money, campus atti-

tudes toward American Indians, and poor academic preparation as reasons for leaving school. Support services, such as professors with a caring attitude, may have prevented their attrition. A second survey of nine enrolled students reported family obligations, time management, lack of money, and distance from home as difficulties. A final survey of nine students in a pre-service education program cited cultural traditions, lack of money, inadequate high school preparation, alcohol and drugs, poor academic advising, and language barriers as impeding their progress.

━━

Mitchell, S., and D. Dell. 1992. The relationship between black students' racial identity and participation in campus organizations. *Journal of College Student Development* 33:39–43.

Cross' research suggests that there are four stages of African American racial identity development: pre-encounter (a belief that African Americans are basically inferior and that values and behavior associated with whites are preferred), encounter (a shift to a pro-African American stand), immersion-emersion (a shift to complete endorsement of African American values and exclusion of white ones), and internalization (selectivity of values of both cultures, association with all oppressed people). This study explores whether students at different stages of racial identity would participate in different kinds of organizations with students at more advanced stages being more likely to participate in culturally-based organizations. The research confirmed the hypothesis about participation in culturally-based organizations, but did not provide significant associations for involvement in non-cultural organizations. An examination of the patterns of involvement in college organizations by African American students suggests that organizational participation meets several different student needs.

━━

Moore, T. L., and C. Reeves-Kazelskis. 1992. Effects of formal instruction on pre-service teachers' beliefs about multicultural education. Paper presented at the annual meeting of the Mid-South Educational Research Association, November, at Knoxville, TN. ERIC, ED 354231.

This study used a pre-test/post-test design to determine the extent to which formal instruction on the topic of multicultural education produces changes in pre-service teachers' beliefs about basic concepts related to the topic. In this case, formal instruction consisted of five hours of lecture and dialogue between two professors of different racial backgrounds. The sample consisted of thirty-one white, female pre-service teachers enrolled in two sections of a practicum course in early childhood education. The pre-service teachers received the instruction in three sessions. Prior to the first lecture session and six weeks after the last one, the education majors responded to the Survey of Multicultural Education Concepts (SMEC). The SMEC is a Likert scale survey designed to assess beliefs and attitudes about multicultural education with items representing racism, sexism, stereotyping, linguistic views, special holidays, and educational practices. According to this study, pre-service teachers did change their beliefs and attitudes during the seven weeks of the study. The authors, therefore, conclude that formal instruction may be used to change some of the beliefs held by pre-service teachers about cultural diversity.

━━

Moran, J., L. Yengo, and A. Algier. 1994. Participation in minority oriented co-curricular organizations. *Journal of College Student Development* 35:143.

The authors report the results of a survey of high-risk African American students about the impact of their involvement in co-curricular activities. Students participating in both African American and non-ethnic organizations report positive ratings on a survey measuring perceived growth in self-awareness and college adjustment. Students participating in the African American organization reported significantly higher gains than students participating in non-ethnic organizations. This brief research suggests the benefits of ethnic-related organizations. The original survey looked at both majority and minority high risk students but only reports on African American students.

Mount Saint Mary's College. 1995. *Many voices: The newsletter of Mount Saint Mary's Multicultural Advisory Council* 4 (2).

Mount Saint Mary's College is involved in actively assessing goals for student outcomes related to diversity. Through campus surveys, students are asked to evaluate what they have learned and the experiences they have had. Results of the assessment are published in *Voices,* the newsletter of the college's Multicultural Advisory Council. In addition, the results are being tracked for all classes over a period of years. These results are also being linked to the many changes on campus, in the curriculum, and in a new freshman seminar which focuses on negotiation, conflict management, and organizational analysis skills. As a result of these new seminars, students of all backgrounds report increased abilities to negotiate a variety of skills related to functioning in a diverse society. The students also relate these increased abilities to a variety of other efforts at Mount Saint Mary's College.

Mow, S. L., and M. T. Nettles. 1993. Minority student access to, and persistence and performance in, college: A review of the trends and research literature. In *Higher education: Handbook of theory and research,* edited by J. C. Smart. New York: Agathon Press.

In this review of the literature the authors discuss the available data on white, African American, Latino/a, American Indian, and Asian American students. They suggest that institutions can improve overall retention rates if students, African American students in particular, are attracted immediately after graduating from high school, and if ways are found to compensate for differences in their preparation for college and their socioeconomic status. Future research approaches are recommended.

Murray, C. B. 1996. Estimating achievement performance: A confirmation bias. *Journal of Black Psychology* 22 (1): 67–85.

This study investigated whether stereotypes biased the way one perceives members of social groups. There were 200 undergraduate subjects, including eighty white, seventy Asian American, and thirty-nine others. The subjects were assigned to one of sixteen experimental conditions and exposed a race by social class by performance design. The subjects viewed a four-minute video of a child that contained race, social class, and gender cues. Half of the participants were shown an additional twelve minute tape of the child responding to twenty-five achievement test problems. The videos was arranged to present an inconsistent picture of the child's ability. The participants were asked to evaluate each child on 16 items forming four clusters: work habits, sociability, emotional maturity, and cognitive skills. In relation to work habits, African American children were rated significantly lower than white children. In relation to sociability,

African American, lower class, male children rated lower than the combined race by social class by gender groups. In regard to emotional maturity, African American, lower class, male children were perceived more negatively. Once again the African American, male children were rated significantly lower than other races by gender groups in cognitive skills. In general the study found that one's race, social class, and gender have an effect on how one is academically evaluated. Race has the most consistent and strongest effect for bias, social class varies according to the traits examined, and gender differences are tempered by race. The author suggests the elimination of structural barriers that perpetuate and reinforce personal stereotypical behavior.

=====

Musil, C. M., ed. 1992. *The courage to question: Women's studies and student learning.* Washington, DC: Association of American Colleges. ERIC, ED 347890.

This book uses ten case studies to examine the impact of women's studies programs on students. These ten institutions represent the diversity of higher education, including public and private; large and small; urban, suburban and rural; coeducational and single sex; research universities and liberal arts colleges; as well as geographic diversity. The different campuses employed a variety of assessment techniques to analyze the impact of the women's studies programs. The purpose of the study was to determine in a systematic way what parts of these programs work and also what undergraduate students find in the programs that makes their experience distinctive and meaningful. In general, results indicate that women's studies programs have succeeded in engaging students intellectually and personally. In terms of the issue of diversity, all participating women's studies programs articulated diversity as an important learning goal.

=====

Musil, C. M., M. García, Y. Moses, and D. G. Smith. 1995. *Diversity in higher education: A work in progress.* Washington, DC: Association of American Colleges and Universities.

This report is an effort to capture some of the central lessons learned from nineteen residential colleges that received Ford Foundation grants in the Campus Diversity Initiative. Although the results of Ford-funded diversity projects were positive, very few participants developed or implemented assessments. The report is divided into six sections, and features an analysis of institutional innovations and how initiatives become institutionalized and examines implications for the future generation of diversity projects.

=====

Myers-Lipton, S. J. 1996. Effect of service-learning on college students' attitudes toward international understanding. *Journal of College Student Development* 37:659–668.

Myers-Lipton looks at ways to measure the creation of critical and engaged learners who will be involved in transformation of the world. He attempts to determine the impact of participation in service-learning programs on the creation of empowered change agents. The study reviewed the differences among three groups of students: those actively engaged in a service-learning project that linked service to academic courses; those engaged in service that was not linked to academic courses; and those who were not participants in any formal service projects. The researcher made efforts to control for the likely attitudes of the self-selected groups that participated in service. All participants were administered the International Understanding Scale, a comprehensive instrument to measure international awareness and understanding. A series of dependent variables measuring awareness, involvement, and commitment to international issues was constructed from this instrument. The independent variables were gender, race (either person of color or white), political orientation, parent education, and participation in a type of service. The changes in global concern and cultural respect were moderate to strong for those students who participated in service-learning compared to those who participated in service alone or did not participate. Although this study looked specifically at international issues, the significant change in levels of cultural respect may be important for broader issues of diversity.

==

Nagasawa, R., and D. J. Espinosa. 1992. Educational achievement and the adaptive strategy of Asian American college students: Facts, theory, and hypotheses. *Journal of College Student Development* 33:137–142.

This article advances a theory on the high level of educational aspiration and achievement of Asian Americans. The authors suggest that Asian Americans seek entry to middle-class status through legitimate structures, but that their aspirations are thwarted by racism. So the Asian American joins a subculture, that of other Asian Americans seeking educational achievement in which their striving is reinforced. Participation in the sub-culture may lead to neglect of the larger group's norms of behavior, leading to a continuing cycle. This hypothesis attempts to make sense of the reality that Asian American students represent a disproportionately large cohort in American higher education, that they frequently associate within their own group, that more recent immigrants are more successful in college, and that in the work world Asian Americans encounter discrimination. The implications for change are that methods to socialize Asian American students to the larger population norms are necessary to break down the subcultures.

==

National Center for Teaching and Learning Assessment. 1995. *Realizing the potential: Improving postsecondary teaching and learning and assessment.* University Park, PA.

This report includes the results of a study of fourteen predominantly public, urban, and commuting institutions. Using case studies, the researchers studied organizational structures, policies, and practices focusing, in part, on the implications for teaching, learning, and assessment.

==

National Task Force for Minority Achievement in Higher Education. 1990. *Achieving campus diversity: Policies for change.* Denver, CO: Education Commission of the States. ERIC, ED 329178.

This study of community colleges defines underrepresentation, presents a conceptual framework for analyzing preparation issues, presents institutional strategies for responding to preparation issues, and discusses the role of leadership in this endeavor. The authors conclude that approaching the issue of student diversity from the perspective of organizational culture can help institutional leaders avoid the pursuit of strategies that promise diminishing returns. They also suggest that a deficiency model as well as an achievement model present complicating factors for the future of community colleges.

Nelson, E. S., and S. L. Krieger. 1997. Changes in attitudes toward homosexuality in college students: Implementation of a gay men and lesbian peer panel. *Journal of Homosexuality* 33 (2): 63–81.

The authors evaluate the effect of a fifty-minute presentation by two male and two female members of a university's lesbian and gay student group on one-hundred ninety students enrolled in six sections of a psychology course. The presentation included the personal stories of each of the students and a question and answer period. Using pre- and post-test methodology, the authors found that men had more negative attitudes, both before and after the presentation, than women. Both men and women had significantly more positive attitudes after the presentation. The authors recommend that differences between the audience and the panel members should be minimal to accentuate their commonality, the encounter should be interactional, and that feedback should be elicited after the intervention.

——

Nelson, N. J., C. Johnson, J. Boyd, and T. Scott. 1994. The effects of participation in an intergroup communication program: An assessment of Shippensburg University's Building Bridges program. Paper presented at the annual meeting of the Eastern Psychological Association, April, at Providence, RI. ERIC, ED 370152.

This study evaluates the impact of a program designed to facilitate communication and understanding among college students from diverse backgrounds. Trained student facilitators led discussions in courses on relevant topics. Following the program, a telephone survey of students in the program as well as a control group measured racial attitudes. Results suggest that after the program white students were more optimistic about intergroup understanding, more comfortable interacting with minority students, and more aware of racial issues.

——

Nelson, W. 1994. Receptivity to institutional assistance: An important variable for African American and Mexican American student achievement. *Journal of College Student Development* 35:378–384.

Nelson looks at academically high-risk students to determine if there is a difference in receptivity to student services and if there is a difference in first year GPA between students who are receptive to services and those who are not. The research is based on studies of two groups of African American and Mexican American/Latino/a students—high ability and at-risk. Both groups of students participated in special programs through the dean of students office at this university. Nelson looks at differential receptivity of students in the groups to academic assistance, career counseling, personal counseling, and social enrichment. The author suggests: at-risk students are more receptive to career counseling than high achievers; successful students in both groups are more receptive to career counseling than unsuccessful students; high achievers are more receptive to academic support; successful at-risk students are more receptive to social enrichment; and successful high achievers are less receptive to social enrichment. Nelson concludes that services to assist students, both at-risk students and high achievers, are generally useful.

Nesbitt, L., Jr., et al. 1994. On racial sensitivity training for college freshmen: A survey of institutional opinions and practices. *Journal of Blacks in Higher Education* (3): 77–79.

A group of educators was asked their opinions on racial sensitivity programs among college freshmen. Some argued that these programs increase racial sensitivity and tolerance. Others suggested they may heighten awareness of racial differences.

═══

Nettles, M. T. 1990a. Success in doctoral programs: Experiences of minority and white students. *American Journal of Education* 98:494–521.

This paper examines the differences among African American, Latino/a, and white doctoral students at four major universities. Post-first year doctoral students in education, the social sciences, humanities, and biological/physical sciences were randomly selected from Florida State University, Rutgers University, Ohio State University, and the University of Maryland at College Park. Of the initial 1352 subjects, 1286 responded to the survey, including 194 African Americans, 92 Latino/as, and 667 whites. After controlling for demographic differences, the study showed that African American doctoral students attended less selective undergraduate institutions, received lower undergraduate GPAs, and were more likely than their Latino/a and white classmates to major in science. African American students from the lower socioeconomic groups received the fewest teaching and research assistantships as compared to their white and Latino/a classmates. It also showed that although Latino/as attended more selective undergraduate institutions than whites, their grades were not significantly different and their fields of study were similar. When African Americans and Latino/as were compared to whites, the African American and Latino/a students perceived their graduate institution as racially discriminatory, received lower doctoral GPAs, perceived greater support from their mentor, and were more satisfied with their doctoral program. In contrast, Latino/as were less likely than white and African American students to take time off after receiving their bachelor's degree before entering their doctoral program, were more likely to receive fellowships or assistantships, were more likely to be full-time students, were more socially involved, and spent more time studying.

═══

——, ed. 1990b. *The effect of assessment on minority student participation.* New Directions for Institutional Research, no. 65. San Francisco: Jossey-Bass.

This monograph includes seven chapters discussing various assessment issues as they relate to minority students. Topics include: assessment issues for minority populations; assessment in specific disciplines; the implications of assessment for recruitment, admissions, and retention; and assessing program effectiveness.

═══

Nettles, M. T., and C. Hudgins. 1995. *An evaluation of Philip Morris Companies, Inc. Tolerance on campus: Establishing common ground.* Colby College and Northern Illinois University.

These reports were produced for the evaluation component of the Philip Morris Initiative, Tolerance on Campus: Establishing Common Ground. The diversity initiative was launched in 1992 with an investment of $1.2 million and the evaluation was executed both to assist Philip Morris in measuring the effectiveness of the initiative and to determine the outcomes of the variety of interventions at the eleven participating institutions. Institutions were evaluated using a seven step multidimensional approach, that included two-day site visits, and analysis of qualitative and quantitative data provided by the institutions. Results of both programs proved positive and are described in the context of each report.

———

Nettles, M. T., A. R. Thoeny, and E. J. Gosman. 1986. Comparative and predictive analyses of black and white students' college achievement and experiences. *Journal of Higher Education* 57:289–318.

Studying over 4,000 African American and white students at thirty campuses, investigators sought to identify differences in college performance, differences in predictors of success, and factors in the college experience which affect success differently for the two groups of students. In addition to the expected role of traditional academic indicators, the analysis revealed an important role for nonacademic predictors such as living on campus, being involved, and for African American students, being in a racial majority.

———

Neville, H., and M. Furlong. 1994. The impact of participation in a cultural awareness program on the racial attitudes and social behaviors of first year college students. *Journal of College Student Development* 35:371–377.

This research measured the impact of three types of treatment on racial attitudes. Students were randomly assigned to a cultural awareness workshop, personal development workshop, or no workshop. The post-test only design was used to reduce the possibility of sensitization that might be caused by a pre-test. After treatment in one of the workshops or as part of the control group, students completed an attitudes and program evaluation questionnaire. The research revealed that participants in cultural awareness workshops do not report more positive racial attitudes toward and social interactions with persons of other groups compared to participants in personal development workshops or the control group. The results suggest that race/ethnicity may be a greater influence on attitudes and behaviors than any kind of treatment. Researchers also found that attrition from the study was high and that incentives for participation were important.

———

Newswanger, J. 1996. Relationship between white racial identity attitudes and the experience of a black college roommate. *Journal of College Student Development* 37:536–542.

White male students at an Ivy League college were administered the white Racial Identity Attitudes Scale. The survey was administered to four groups of students: students in each class who had been randomly assigned African American roommates in their first year of college; randomly selected freshmen; randomly selected seniors; and residential advisers. Although the roommate group did indicate extended interracial conversation, members of that group reported the least comfort in interactions with African Americans. Members of the roommate group reported the highest number of positive and negative changes in thinking about race. The varied responses brought the mean response to that of other groups. This study does not suggest any significant benefit to intentional mixed-race roommate matching, unless other programs and activities are used to build on the chance nature of roommate pairing.

Nora, A. 1987. Determinants of retention among Chicano college students: A struc-
    tural model. *Research in Higher Education* 26:31–59.
This study tested a modified version of Tinto's student attrition model on a Latino/a
student population in two year colleges. Structural equation modeling and LISREL VI
were used to examine the parameter estimates of the structural and measurement models of the causal model. Measures of goodness of fit were examined to provide indices
of the overall fit of the causal model in the study. The measurement and structural
models were found to represent a plausible causal model of student retention among
Latino/a students. Although the measurements used in assessing the fit of the model
reflected the overall strength of the hypothesized model, the present study was not
entirely supportive of Tinto's model. The findings were only minimally supportive of
the hypothesized relationship between measures of academic integration and retention.
The results indicated that the hypothesized relationship between measures of social
integration could not be substantiated. Moreover, measures of initial commitments
were found to have a significantly large direct effect on the dependent variable, retention.

———. 1990. Campus-based aid programs as determinants of retention among Hispanic
    community college students. *Journal of Higher Education* 61:312–331.
The author looked at the impact of financial aid on the retention and persistence of
Latino/a students in community colleges. Prior research on retention, while including
financial aid as a factor, often looked at four-year colleges and universities and did not
include financial aid as a significant variable. Because Latino/a students are disproportionately represented in community colleges, this research may offer important
information on this group. The study looked at a cohort of students at one community
college in Texas with a significant Latino/a population in a community with a low medi-
an family income. The author used structural equation modeling to examine the impact
of financial aid on student retention and persistence. The research showed that non-
campus-based resources (Pell grants) and campus-based resources (SEOGs, CWS,
and NDSLs) had significant effect on retention. Other factors such as high school
grades and college GPA were significant, but not as strong as the impact of various
financial aid elements. With recent government discussions about the amount of type
of student financial aid, this is important research to consider.

———. 1993. Two-year colleges and minority students' educational aspirations: Help or
    hindrance? In *Higher education: Handbook of theory and research.* New York:
    Agathon Press.
This study presents a review of the literature on minorities and community colleges
that are theoretically or literature based. The study also includes a listing of some of
the factors from the literature that associate with minority retention and correspond to
persistence-related intervention strategies.

Nora, A., and A. Cabrera. 1996. The role of perceptions of prejudice and discrimina-
    tion on the adjustment of minority students to college. *Journal of Higher Education*
    67:119–148.
This study assessed the role of perceptions of prejudice and discrimination in college
persistence. The study showed that minorities and non-minorities alike perceived a

negative campus climate, discriminatory attitudes held by faculty and staff, and negative racial experiences in the classroom. Perceptions of prejudice and discrimination negatively affected the adjustment of minority students.

═══

Nora, A., A. Hagedorn, A. Cabrera, and E. T. Pascarella. 1994. Differential impacts of academic and social experiences on college-related behavioral outcomes across different ethnic and gender groups at four-year institutions. Paper presented at the annual meeting of the American Educational Research Association, April, at New Orleans, LA.

Twenty-six two and four-year, private and public, commuter and residential colleges were asked to participate in this study which attempts to examine the cognitive, affective, and environmental factors that influence persistence. Thirty-nine hundred students filled out four instruments designed to collect data. Results indicate that academic achievement and persistence are strongly related to each other, and suggest that tutoring, study groups, and academic counseling are perhaps the most useful interventions. For minority students, dropping out is strongly associated with family responsibilities and working off-campus, factors which are not negated by strong peer and faculty relationships or academic experiences. For women, however, faculty mentoring and non-classroom interaction with faculty prove to have a significant positive impact on persistence.

═══

Nottingham, C. R., D. H. Rosen, and C. Parks. 1992. Psychological well-being among African American university students. *Journal of College Student Development* 33:356–362.

This study examines the differences in psychological well-being between African American students at a predominantly black university (PBU) and a predominantly white university (PWU). Students completed a variety of scales and inventories. After controlling for socioeconomic status, the study showed no significant differences between students at the PWU and PBU in measures of hopelessness, suicidal ideation, alienation, meaninglessness, powerlessness, or depression. However, students at the PBU showed higher positive and total stress scores than did PWU students, and PWU students scored higher in Cross' immersion-emersion racial identity stage. Analyses also showed stronger feelings of alienation were associated with depressive symptoms, higher levels of hopelessness, lower self esteem, and higher pre-encounter racial identity scores. Students enrolled at the PWU reported less adequate information about African American subjects available on campus, higher levels of isolation, and higher levels of ethnocentrism.

═══

Office of Academic Multicultural Initiatives. 1994. *The Michigan study project.* Ann Arbor: University of Michigan.

The Michigan study was begun in 1990 to undertake a comprehensive study of the impact of the university's multicultural and diversity efforts. The major element is a longitudinal study of the undergraduate class of 1994. Survey data each year were complemented by interviews. The initial findings describe the expectations and experiences of students from a variety of backgrounds as they go through the university. While the full results are not yet available, preliminary results highlight the differing perceptions students have about diversity initiatives, as well as the potential impact that curricular efforts hold to improve student attitudes about diversity and understandings of equity issues in society.

═══

Okazaki, S., and S. Stanley. 1995. Methodological issues in assessment research with ethnic minorities. *Psychological Assessment* 7:367–75.
The authors discuss the use of ethnicity as a variable in assessment research. They suggest that the assumptions of researchers about the characteristics of ethnicity should be made clear in the research. This is a useful article for those undertaking research using ethnicity as an independent variable.

═══

Olivas, M. A. 1993. The attack on affirmative action: Lives in parallel universes. *Change* 25 (2): 16–20.
This essay, which is based on a longer law journal article, places conservative attacks on affirmative action in the context of the history of racial discrimination which affirmative action was intended to remedy. The author, a professor of law, provides a brief overview of the major court cases which brought about desegregation in higher education and addresses issues related to the use of standardized test scores in admission decisions at law schools and other types of institutions.

═══

Ortíz, A. M. 1995. Promoting racial understanding in college students: A study of educational and developmental interventions. Paper presented at the annual meeting of the Association for the Study of Higher Education, November, at Orlando, FL.
Qualitative methods, including semi-structured interviews and participant observation, were used to explore the educational interventions successful in promoting racial understanding in the group of college students studied. The study focuses on the cognitive developmental differences in the effectiveness of activities and interventions. Findings indicate that the influence of informal peer interaction and peer-led discussions in class were effective for all students, but especially for first-year students who preferred this as the primary vehicle for learning about multicultural issues. Fourth-year students found that instructor-led discussions and activities were most effective for them and supported and preferred instructors playing a large role in educational interventions. Supplemental and required readings were also found to be highly effective in promoting racial understanding in these students. The results of this study also suggest that students with prior experiences with discrimination and racism have much higher expectations for educational interventions, trainers, and instructors. These students found that their peers were better sources of information than instructors or trainers. The evidence generally supports the notion that the development of racial understanding mimics an established framework of cognitive development in college students, with the surprising exception that seniors prefer instructor-led activities. Although the study is exploratory, it does offer insight to the delicate nature of delivering educational interventions into the area of multiculturalism and diversity.

═══

Osajima, K. 1995. Racial politics and the invisibility of Asian Americans in higher education. *Educational Foundations* 9 (1): 35–53.
This qualitative study examines issues of invisibility of Asian American students through institutional and political practices at twelve different institutions of higher

education. Although Asian American invisibility is changing, according to the author, institutional neglect is far from moot.

===

Pascarella, E. T., M. I. Edison, A. Nora, L. S. Hagedorn, and P. T. Terenzini. 1996a. Additional evidence on the cognitive effects of college racial composition: A research note. *Journal of College Student Development* 37:494–501.

The researchers here expand on earlier research on the impact of attendance at historically black colleges. Earlier research had been limited by a short time-span and limited control for confounding variables. This research considers a variety of initial factors and looks at a cohort of students after two years of college. The groups compared are African American students attending historically black colleges and African Americans attending predominantly white colleges. The dependent variables are scores on writing skills and science reasoning tests administered at the end of the second year of college. Environmental factors such as measured pre-college ability, gender, age, residence, number of papers written, and academic experiences were used as covariates. Analysis of covariance shows a significantly higher score on writing skills for students attending an historically black college and no significant difference for students attending an historically black college on science reasoning. Additional analysis suggests that African American students attending an historically black college have an advantage over African American students at a predominantly white college of approximately one-third standard deviation. This research confirms prior findings on the benefits for African American students of attending historically black colleges and suggests that much might be learned from those institutions that could be applied to predominantly white institutions. Generalizations should be made with caution as the research only looks at two historically black colleges and sixteen predominantly white colleges. Also, the time commitment required may have limited the kinds of students who participated.

===

——. 1996b. Influences on students' openness to diversity and challenge in the first year of college. *Journal of Higher Education* 67:174–195.

This multi-institutional study sought to determine the factors influencing students' openness to diversity and challenge during the first year of college. Controlling for student background characteristics and other confounding influences, a non-discriminatory racial environment, on-campus residence, participation in a racial or cultural awareness workshop, and extent of involvement with diverse peers had positive effects on openness to diversity/challenge. Conversely, Greek affiliation had a negative effect.

===

Pascarella, E. T., E. J. Whitt, M. I. Edison, A. Nora, L. S. Hagedorn, P. M. Yeager, and P. T. Terenzini. 1997. Women's perceptions of a "chilly climate" and their cognitive outcomes during the first year of college. *Journal of College Student Development* 38:109–124.

This study looks at students at twenty two- and four-year institutions. The hypothesis of the study is that there is a correlation between a perceived "chilly" campus climate for women and impaired cognitive growth of women during the first year. There seems to be significant potential negative cognitive effects for women at two-year colleges.

Pascarella, E. T., E. J. Whitt, A. Nora, M. Edison, L. S. Hagedorn, and P. T. Terenzini. 1996. What have we learned from the first year of the National Study of Student Learning? *Journal of College Student Development* 37:182–192.

This article summarizes some of the major findings from the first year of the federally funded National Study of Student Learning and discusses the implications of those findings for higher education policy and practice. Eighteen four-year and five two-year postsecondary institutions participated, yielding a sample of 3,840 students from which data here gathered in 1992; 2,685 students participated in a 1993 follow up study. Results of the survey indicate that racial or cultural awareness workshops can foster student openness to cultural, racial, and value diversity. Other findings suggest that openness to diversity and challenge was positively influenced by a nondiscriminatory racial environment. This suggests that institutions can facilitate student growth on this dimension.

Pence, D. 1992. A women's studies course: Its impact on women's attitudes toward men and masculinity. *National Women's Studies Association Journal* 4:321–335.

The author hypothesizes that few men take women's studies courses because they lack interest in the topic or because, as is widely believed, women do not want men in these classes. To ascertain whether women in women's studies classes are hostile toward men, the researcher designed a study to measure how women's attitudes toward men differ among those enrolled in an introductory women's studies course and those enrolled in an introductory sociology course. The results of the study indicate that attitudes toward men improved for the women in the women's studies course. Based on these data, the author concludes that women's studies courses are falsely perceived as hostile to men and may, in fact, help women to better understand and appreciate men.

Person, D., and M. Christensen. 1996. Understanding black student culture and black student retention. *NASPA Journal* 34:47–56.

The authors observed African American student culture at a liberal arts college in Eastern Pennsylvania and an engineering institution. Ninety-three students were contacted by mail and thirty-nine responded. Twenty-seven males and fourteen females of traditional college age participated. All respondents indicated there was a need for "an identifiable African American community" and more institutional support programs for African American students. Eighty-three percent of the students revealed that they spent most of their free time with other African American students and that they had experienced racial discrimination. All students reported that they were satisfied with their academic experiences and that they were more satisfied in their academic settings than in social settings. However, fewer than 50 percent indicated that they were comfortable with faculty members. Fifty-five percent of the students stated that they felt comfortable in their college town, but 82 percent revealed that they felt most at ease at African American Student Union meetings.

Pettigrew, T. F. 1994. Prejudice and discrimination on the college campus. *The HEES Review* 6 (1) [online]. Available at http://www.review.org/issues/vol6no1.html.

Pettigrew summarizes the results of decades of research suggesting that equal status, common goals, institutional support, and the opportunity for minority and majority group members to interact as individuals facilitate successful intergroup contact. Also discussed are the definition and relationship of prejudice to discrimination, the critical importance of situational norms, four social psychological processes underlying normative change, moving from desegregation to integration, and a number of helpful references.

═══

Phelps, R., C. Potter, R. Slavick, J. Day, and L. Poloven. 1996. Roommate satisfaction and ethnic pride in same race and mixed race university roommate pairs. *Journal of College Student Development* 37:377–387.

One hundred and one same-race and mixed-race, randomly assigned roommate pairs at the University of Georgia were used in assessing roommate satisfaction and ethnic pride. The results indicated African American roommate pairs were significantly more satisfied than mixed-race pairs. African Americans also had the highest ethnic pride score. The importance of this study lies in the well-documented issue of African Americans feeling isolated and alienated on predominantly white campuses. The relationship of non-mixed roommates may lead to African American students' increased sense of affirmation and satisfaction at predominantly white institutions.

═══

Piskur, J., and D. Degelman. 1992. Effect of reading a summary of research about biological bases of homosexual orientation on attitudes toward homosexuals. *Psychological Reports* 7:1219–1225.

This study asks if attitudes toward homosexuals change when information about the biological basis of homosexuality is presented. Readings that give a biological explanation for homosexuality were distributed to one of three groups. The second group had a different explanation for homosexuality and the third group had no reading. Among women the biological explanation seemed to engender a positive attitude toward homosexuals.

═══

Powers, S. M. 1996. An implementation study of hypermedia-based multicultural training. Ed.D. dissertation, University of Virginia. Abstract in *Dissertation Abstracts International* 57 (08): 3467A.

This dissertation examines the impact of a hypermedia-based computer program on the knowledge and awareness of multicultural issues as well as on the interactions of students. The program was applied to three groups of undergraduate students: individually; in pairs; and in facilitated discussions. The research group was composed of sixty-five undergraduate students. The questions asked were: does the method of using the program impact students' knowledge and awareness of multicultural issues; does the method of using the program affect the interactions among students; and how do students report their engagement with the program? The impact of the program was measured through a pre- and post-treatment survey to measure student awareness and knowledge. Students were also observed during their use of the computer program and a sample of the students was interviewed. Of the three methods of use, the facilitated discussion resulted in the greatest impact on students' knowledge and awareness. In general, all students who used the program reported that it was an effective tool and that they especially liked the games and music portions of the program.

Rembert, W. I., S. L. Calvert, and J. A. Watson. 1986. Effects of an academic summer camp experience on black students' high school scholastic performance and subsequent college attendance decisions. *College Student Journal* 20:374–384.

The effectiveness of a summer camp for academic development on the performance of African American high school students was tested at Winthrop College in South Carolina by matching eighty-seven students who attended the camp with a control group of fifty-five students who did not attend. The Comprehensive Test of Basic Skills (CTBS) was completed by both groups, and the experimental group completed the Woodcock-Johnson Psycho-Educational Achievement and Interest Tests. Analysis of variance revealed that the experimental-group students scored higher on all CTBS measures than did the control group. No gender differences were found among the experimental-group students on either the CTBS or the Woodcock-Johnson tests. Of the students who had graduated from high school, more than twice as many of the experimental-group students as the control-group students enrolled in college, and 61 percent of the experimental-group students versus 16 percent of the control-group students enrolled in predominantly white institutions. Among high school seniors, more of the experimental-group students than of the control-group students planned to enroll in college (71 percent versus 61 percent) and planned to enroll in a predominantly white institution (51 percent versus 33 percent).

====

Retention programs: A bridge to success for at-risk students. 1994. *Journal of Developmental Education* 17 [special issue].

This journal issue contains descriptions of four exemplary retention programs: the University of California-Berkeley's Summer Bridge Program serving minority students targeted for admission through affirmative action programs; Rutgers University's for-credit Gateway courses designed by faculty members in ten departments for students with low scores on English and mathematics placement tests; Rutgers University's pre-college summer programs offering on-campus residence and faculty interaction to conditionally admitted high school students; and the University of South Carolina's Freshman Seminar, a for-credit course providing orientation, skills training, and a sense of community for entering students.

====

Rhodes, G. S. 1994. The development of a diversity program and an analysis of its effectiveness in altering racial attitudes of students in a freshman orientation course. Ed.D. dissertation, University of Louisville. Abstract in *Dissertation Abstracts International* 55 (07): 1902A.

This study looks at the effects of a program on racial attitudes as part of a new student orientation program. Students in treatment and control groups were asked to complete two scales, one measuring the comfort of whites on encountering African Americans in positions of prestige and intimacy, and the other measuring the acceptance by whites of discrimination against African Americans in public situations. No significant differences were identified between the treatment and control groups on either scale. There were significant differences in responses on the two scales based on such background variables as neighborhood, gender, and father's socio-economic status.

Rice, K. L. 1996. Building bridges: The experience of anti-racist pedagogy. Ph.D. dissertation, University of Maryland, College Park. Abstract in *Dissertation Abstracts International* 57 (07): 2902A.

This dissertation reports on interviews with seven students who participated in a one-semester course, Education and Racism. Interviewees included white and African American students and a very small number of Asian American students. There were no Latino/a or American Indian students in the class. The results indicate that white students developed a new understanding of the existence and issues of racism and African American students developed a voice to express their feelings. Because so few Asian American students were in the class, they reported feelings of being silenced. The nature of this research and the small sample size precludes adoption of the course as a "successful" model for dealing with diversity issues. Rather, the themes that emerge from the conversations with the students might prove useful to those developing courses and other programs on their own campuses.

Rice, R. L. 1991. An intervention program for older-than-average students. *Journal of College Student Development* 32:88–89.

This brief report discusses a simple program to assist students in feeling a connection with the institution. Volunteers contacted older students by telephone at key points during the semester to check on their progress, remind them of important deadlines, and find out if they had any questions. Students who were contacted in this way reported feeling less isolated and more a part of the institution.

Richardson, R. C., Jr. 1989. Changing organizational culture to accommodate student diversity. Paper presented at a meeting of the Society for College and University Planning, at Denver, CO.

Ten public universities in eight states served as case studies for an analysis of the effect of state policy, institutional mission, and organizational culture on the achievement of African American, Latino/a, and American Indian students. Open-ended interviews were conducted with several individuals (e.g. the president, deans, student affairs staff members, and faculty members) at each institution and with a total of 108 African American, Latino/a, and American Indian graduates of the ten universities. Interviews also were conducted with representatives of state governing and/or coordinating boards and personnel of public schools, community colleges, and community-based programs in the communities in which the ten universities were located. From these interviews, a model of institutional adaptation to student diversity was developed that accounted for the state policy environment, institutional mission, and organizational climate. The universities were at one of three stages in improving equity outcomes: an emphasis on increasing student diversity carried out mostly by the student affairs staff; an attempt to cope with the high attrition rates and dissatisfaction produced in the first stage; and a fundamental shift in the organizational culture brought about with intensive faculty involvement. Moving institutions through these three stages requires strong leadership and action in the areas of strategic planning, coordination and control of implementation activities, articulation with community colleges, hiring and tenure procedures, faculty rewards and incentives, student recruitment, and cultural awareness.

———. 1991. *Promoting fair college outcomes: Learning from the experiences of the past decade.* Denver, CO: Education Commission of the States. ERIC, ED 329179.

Case studies of ten public colleges and universities with good records for graduating African Americans, Latino/as, or American Indians were used to develop a survey containing thirty-six state and sixty-eight institutional practices associated with high or improved equity outcomes during the 1980s. Ten states and all of the 142 public, four-year institutions responded to the survey, providing information about the intensity and duration of these practices between 1980 and 1988. States and institutions also provided participation and graduation rates for the racial and ethnic groups they served. Differences in institutional practices explained much of why some institutions got better results than others. The outcomes achieved by some of the public institutions within the ten states, as well as the way that administrative commitment and strategic planning offset the negative consequences of state quality initiatives, demonstrated clearly that diversity and quality need not be pursued as mutually exclusive objectives. Given a supportive state climate, committed leadership, and systematic interventions, institutions can attain both.

══

Richardson, R. C., Jr., and E. F. Skinner. 1990a. *Achieving quality and diversity: Universities in a multicultural society.* New York: Macmillan. ERIC, ED 327093.

Much of the research on institutions which have been successful with diverse student populations has focused on relatively small residential institutions. This book examines ten relatively large, historically white state, commuter colleges and universities which have been identified as successful in graduating African American, Latino/a and/or American Indian students at rates which exceed state and national averages. The ten undisguised case studies are reviewed within a framework of access and quality issues, institutional adaptation to external pressures for improved diversity, and an overview of state- and system-level influences working on the institution. The process of institutional change in each profiled institution is examined through the roles of student affairs in providing a supportive environment; academic affairs in modifying the learning environment; central administration in planning, coordinating and monitoring adaptation; and state coordinating and governing boards in establishing policy conducive to quality and diversity. The work is particularly useful as a study of institutional change within the context of the types of institutions—publicly supported comprehensive universities—which enroll the largest numbers of students from the target groups.

══

———. 1990b. Adapting to diversity: Organizational influences on student achievement. *Journal of Higher Education* 61:485–511.

The experiences of ten public universities that had positive records for enrolling African American, Latino/a, or American Indian students support an adaptation model as the most useful approach to understanding successful efforts to accommodate a more diverse student body without relinquishing traditionally held values related to quality. In this model, the state policy environment, institutional mission and practices, and the dimensions of student diversity all play a part. For example, a ranking of the colleges according to their success in both enrolling and graduating minority students is fairly similar to the ranking of the states in the amount of influence they exert on minority participation and degree achievement. Institutional interventions by the central administration, academic affairs, and student affairs are all a part of the organizational culture that affects student diversity and achievement. Minority students are more likely to enroll if they have adequate preparation, both in terms of expectations about higher education, and experiences similar to the college experience, and if they believe higher education will be helpful in achieving desired adult roles. Their progress will be affected whether or not they follow traditional full-time patterns of college attendance and whether or not they enter college with adult roles and responsibilities. If universities are to achieve both quality and diversity, they must consider a complex set of factors that include the historical relationship with the minority populations they serve. Interventions focused on changing students or buffering them from adverse institutional practices are not sufficient; instead a modification of internal environments to facilitate achievement by diverse learners is required.

===

Riordan, C. 1992. Single- and mixed-gender colleges for women: Educational, attitudinal, and occupational outcomes. *Review of Higher Education* 15:327–346.
This study uses the National Longitudinal Study of the High School Class of 1972 to trace the outcomes of women who graduated from women's colleges (or attended for two years) compared to an equivalent sample of women from mixed-gender colleges. Students who attended women's colleges for at least two years were found to attain significantly more education and higher occupational prestige than women who similarly attended mixed-gender colleges after controlling for entering socio-economic status, cognitive ability, and regional factors. Measures of marital happiness, self-esteem, and locus-of-control factors, again after controls, showed no difference. Graduates of women's colleges compared to graduates of coeducational colleges completed significantly less post-graduate education, yet attained higher occupational prestige, after controls.

===

Ripon College. 1995. Informal communication, information available from the dean of faculty, Ripon, WI.
With the assistance of external funding, Ripon College and Fisk University recently held a conference entitled "Talking about Race as an American Experience." The colleges entered this dialogue because of their similarities—small student bodies, adherence to a liberal arts tradition, and historical roots in the Congregational Church—and their differences—a primarily white tradition at Ripon and African American tradition at Fisk. Preparation for the conference included readings and a survey about racial and other attitudes. The survey revealed the vastly different ways the two communities view race. White Ripon students tended not to think of race when thinking about themselves in relation to others, whereas Fisk students considered race first. These data provided important information for the conversations which followed. Evaluations of the conference and its impact on participants were quite positive and further Fisk and Ripon efforts are being planned.

===

Robbins, S. B., and L. C. Smith. 1993. Enhancement programs for entering university majority and minority freshmen. *Journal of Counseling and Development* 71:510–514.
In this study, the authors evaluate the effects of two enhancement programs for minority and white entering freshmen. The sample comprised 175 students who filled out

pre-test and post-test questionnaires. Results indicate that minorities had greater satisfaction ratings and awareness of individual differences. Students showed improved
adjustment regardless of treatment condition, suggesting comparable effects for a
ten-week classroom-structured adjustment program.

===

Rose, M. 1989. *Lives on the boundary: The struggles and achievements of America's underprepared.* New York: The Free Press. ERIC, ED 310217.
This highly personal work explores the lives, struggles, and successes of underprepared
students in American higher education through the use of case studies and autobiography. The author himself qualifies as a case study for this work, progressing from the
"vocational" track in high school to a faculty position at UCLA. Various contexts are
described in which underprepared students come to grips with the demands placed on
them by higher education, particularly in the area of writing. The most successful is
one in which students are in constant close contact with instructors and tutors, and in
which they have the freedom to make mistakes and explore and express their ideas—
a sort of "honors college for the underprepared."

===

Runyan, M. K. 1991. The effect of extra time on reading comprehension scores for university students with and without learning disabilities. *Journal of Learning
Disabilities* 24 (2): 104–108.
Runyan compares the performance of 16 students with learning disabilities and 15 normally achieving students on tests of reading comprehension and reading rate. Under
timed conditions, students with learning disabilities scored significantly lower than the
normally achieving group. Yet, when each group was given extra time, no differences
in performance appeared.

===

St. John, E. P. 1991. The impact of student financial aid: A review of recent research.
Journal of Student Financial Aid 21 (1): 18–32.
The role of student financial assistance in access and retention issues, particularly for
first-generation college students, is widely acknowledged but seldom studied at the
national level. This literature review, focusing on research from the mid- to late-1980s,
looks at econometric studies of the effects of student aid in a number of areas including access, choice of school, persistence, choice of major, and returns to education. Not
surprisingly, the research supports the notion that student financial assistance has a
positive impact on access to and persistence in higher education, and to broaden the
range of institutions students consider. A major theme of this review is the effect the
shift in student financial aid from grants to loans during the decade of the 1980s will
have on the demonstrated benefits of student aid. Increased proportions of loan aid relative to grants has been found to negatively influence students' decisions to attend college, to persist, and to choose among a wide range of institutions.

===

Sandoval, P. 1990. The evaluation of minority/disadvantaged programs in a state university program. Paper presented at the annual meeting of the American
Educational Research Association, April, at Boston, MA.
This paper describes the methodologies and implementation of minority/disadvantaged
program evaluation across institutions in a large state university system. The ultimate
purpose of the evaluation is to enhance the success of institutions in recruiting, retain-

ing, and graduating students from underrepresented groups in the University of Wisconsin system. The thirteen universities in the system had a total enrollment in 1988 of 162,330. Although the evaluation provided evidence that enrollment of underrepresented students has increased, few efforts have been made by the system to compare past retention to current retention rates. Several institutions have reported success with state-funded tutorial programs and projects designed to retain minority students. The article offers recommendations for improving the evaluation methodology.

═══

Santa Rita, E., and J. B. Bacote. 1996. *The benefits of College Discovery Prefreshman Summer Program for minority and low income students*. Bronx, NY: City University of New York, Bronx Community College. ERIC, ED 394536.

This research report describes the College Discovery Prefreshman Summer Program (CDPSP) at Bronx Community College. During this six-week program, students of color receive intensive instruction in English, reading and mathematics, career counseling, and study skills preparation. In 1993, fifty-two participants' academic progress was tracked. The forty-two students who responded to the surveys revealed that, in general, students rated the program high for meeting their academic and non-academic goals. Asian American students, however, did not feel that the program met their academic and non-academic goals. Participants rated the CDPSP preparation high. The mean grade point average of 2.64 fell slightly, but rose by the end of the year. Ninety-three percent of the CDPSP participants persisted to their third semester.

═══

Santiago, I. S. 1996. Increasing the Latino leadership pipeline: Institutional and organizational strategies. In *Achieving administrative diversity*, edited by I. H. Johnson and A. J. Ottens. New Directions for Student Services, no. 74. San Francisco: Jossey-Bass.

The author reviews the literature on the Latino/a experience in college. In order for institutions to teach students about diversity, they must employ more staff from Latino/a and other ethnic minority groups. This goal will require institutional commitment to multiculturalism in all practices as well as in the curriculum. A diverse campus cannot be created without a diverse faculty and staff. The author supports this claim by highlighting the success of Hostos Community College. For two decades, Hostos has been successful in attracting qualified faculty and administrators from diverse ethnic backgrounds. As a result, Hostos has ranked among the top two institutions in higher education to graduate Latino/a students.

═══

Sax, L. 1996. The dynamics of "tokenism": How college students are affected by the proportion of women in their major. *Research in Higher Education* 37:389–425.

National and longitudinal data were utilized to determine whether the proportion of women in a major had any impact on students in the same major. The results showed that the proportion of women in the major did not have any effect on students' grades in college, satisfaction with their major, academic self-concept, mathematical self-concept, or social self-concept.

Schoem, D. 1996. Intergroup relations, conflict, and community. In *Democratic education in an age of difference: Redefining citizenship in higher education.* edited by R.
Guarasci and G. H. Cornwell. San Francisco: Jossey-Bass.
Schoem describes the design and impact on students of the University of Michigan's
program on intergroup relations, conflict, and community. The program is designed as
an intentional part of a liberal arts curriculum to address intergroup ignorance and dis-
trust, community building, and discourse. There is an academic component as well as
a co-curricular approach.

Schoem, D., L. Frankel, X. Zúñiga, and E. Lewis, eds. 1995. *Multicultural teaching in
the university.* Westport, CT: Praeger.
This book contains more than twenty chapters related to multicultural teaching. The
authors engage issues of design, approaches which facilitate student learning, and challenges that emerge when one is trying to set conditions for learning on a challenging
and charged topic. Most chapters include some form of evaluation or reflections on the
impact on students. Several chapters focus on "roundtable discussions" on multicultural teaching and learning.

Schwalm, K. T. 1995. Providing computer conferencing opportunities for minority students and measuring results. Proceedings of the 1995 Annual Convention of the
Association for Educational Communications and Technology. ERIC, ED
383335.
This paper reviews the computer backgrounds and the short- and long-range success
of students of color at Glendale Community College in Arizona over a two-year period. The findings show that Asian American and white students were over-represented
among the users of an Internet Relay Chat. A sixteen-item annotated bibliography and
various tables are included.

Sedlacek, W. E. 1994. Issues in advancing diversity through assessment. *Journal of
Counseling and Development* 72:549–553.
This report discusses five problems related to diversity that exist in the counseling and
personnel professions. A discussion of how those concerned with assessment can
address each problem is presented, as are overall suggestions for change, such as joint
training programs and projects among professional groups.

———. 1995a. *Improving racial and ethnic diversity and campus climate at four-year independent Midwest colleges: An evaluation report of the Lilly Endowment Grant Program.*
College Park: University of Maryland.
This evaluation was designed to encourage and assist institutions in successfully retaining minority students for the full course of the baccalaureate degree. This is an evaluation report of Lilly Foundation-funded initiatives on thirty campuses. Several direct
and indirect changes on campus are directly attributable to the Lilly initiative, including course revisions, changes in curriculum and library materials, hiring of nontraditional faculty and staff, greater involvement of administration and trustees in diversity
issues, ability to train faculty and students on diversity issues, and increased awareness
of diversity issues.

——. 1995b. Using research to reduce racism at a university. *Journal of Humanistic Education and Development* 33 (3): 131–140.

This essay reports on the uses of long-term research on issues of racism and discrimination at a large public university. What is especially interesting and valuable about this report is its detail of how the author's twenty-five year history of research was used to assist the university in defending its activities in support of diversity, specifically, a race-specific scholarship program developed to increase representation of African American students. The scholarship program was challenged by a student of another minority group who claimed that it was created to solve a problem that no longer exists. The author's history of research was used by the university to demonstrate the need to continue and even broaden such programs to address needs of other minority groups.

===

Sharma, M. P., and J. S. Mulka. 1993. The impact of international education upon United States students in comparative perspective. Paper presented at the annual meeting of the Comparative and International Education Society, March, at Kingston, Jamaica. ERIC, ED 358800.

This study was designed to answer two research questions: does on-campus population density of international students have an impact on U. S. students' international attitudes; and does the involvement of the university in study abroad programs have an impact on U. S. students' international attitudes? To answer these questions, researchers randomly surveyed U. S. students at six American universities that were identified as having different densities of international students and different levels of involvement in study abroad programs. An instrument was developed which evaluated student attitudes in seven areas including cultural pluralism, world-mindedness, international career aspirations, and political liberalism. The forty-two item questionnaire was distributed to 2,400 students. In general, the results indicate that the higher the interaction level with international students, the more positive the attitudes of U. S. students.

===

Sheared, V. 1994. Giving voice: An inclusive model of instruction—A womanist perspective. In *Confronting racism and sexism*, edited by E. Hayes and S. A. J. Colin, III. New Directions for Adult and Continuing Education, no. 61. San Francisco: Jossey-Bass.

This article reviews the literature on the "womanist" perspective, which recognizes that gender and class complicate the lives of students. Through utilizing diverse voices in instruction, the author challenges educators to redefine the role of education. In a course entitled Educating Disadvantaged Adults, the author asked students to be accountable for what they learn and to come up with a new title for the course. Students worked alone in small groups to uncover their own biases and to define who they consider disadvantaged, based on the readings and discussions. At the end of the course, each student presented his or her new title and fielded questions from classmates. The author found that all students had changed their definition about who is disadvantaged. Also, the research revealed that students began to connect with issues that they had learned about and began to use "we" instead of "them and us." Students came to understand how their political, economic, social, and historical being is connected to their race, gender, and class status.

Sia, A. P., and D. Mosher. 1994. Perception of multicultural concepts by preservice teachers in two institutions. Paper presented at the annual meeting of the Association of Teacher Educators, February, at Atlanta, GA. ERIC, ED 367603.
This paper presents the results of a study of pre-service teachers' beliefs about cultural sensitivity, prejudices, and multicultural education at two universities. The study participants included forty-five students enrolled in teaching methods courses at California State University—Northridge and Pacific Lutheran University. The methods courses did not deal directly with multicultural concepts, although the students conducted field site visits in "diverse" educational settings during the semester of the study. All participants had previously taken coursework that included elements of multicultural education. In general, respondents at both institutions indicated a high degree of cultural sensitivity in both pre- and post-tests. In fact, there was no significant change between measurements. In general, respondents were very positive about multicultural education, indicating that it can instill knowledge about, respect for, and acceptance of all cultures. Respondents conceptualized multicultural education partly as reformative and partly as an additive process.

=

Sidel, R. 1994. *Battling bias: The struggle for identity and community on college campuses.* New York: Viking Penguin.
Sidel chronicles the experiences of students throughout the U. S. dealing with discrimination and identity on college campuses. While definitive conclusions are not sought or presented, the voices of the students are clear, articulate, honest, and optimistic. The book richly describes the processes employed by students to successfully navigate today's multicultural campuses.

=

Smith, D. G. 1989. *The challenge of diversity: Involvement or alienation in the academy?* ASHE-ERIC Higher Education Report, no. 5. Washington, DC: George Washington University, School of Education.
This monograph provides a good introduction to the study of diversity in higher education. Beginning with a description of the current state of enrollments, graduation rates, campus climates, and a review of theoretical perspectives which may be useful, Smith examines patterns emerging from studies of institutions which have been labeled successful. An examination of the organizational implications of diversity, suggests that successful institutional organization for diversity goes beyond simply making accommodations for students, in fact, requiring a reframing of the basic questions institutions ask themselves about mission, values, dealing with conflict, and what constitutes institutional quality.

=

——. 1990. Women's colleges and coed colleges: Is there a difference for women? *Journal of Higher Education* 61:181–197.
Using data from the Cooperative Institutional Research Project of 1982 and a follow-up survey, Smith compares responses of women who attended women's colleges and women who attended coeducational colleges on the degree to which they perceived they had changed over four years. In addition, Smith measures respondants' satisfaction with the institution, their educational aspirations, and their perception of institutional goals and values. Regression analysis suggests that women who attended women's colleges rated their institutions more positively on measures of academic pro-

gram and contact with faculty and administration, as well as perceived changes in values of tolerance and cultural awareness. Persistence to graduation was also higher. Social life was rated lower, however. The study's implications for a theory of involvement in education as a crucial element in student success are discussed.

====

Smith, D. G., L. E. Wolf, and T. Levitan, eds. 1994. *Studying diversity in higher education.* New Directions for Institutional Research, no. 81. San Francisco: Jossey-Bass.

The seven chapters in this volume examine the issue of studying diversity from the point of view of the practicing institutional researcher. The introduction by the editors outlines basic issues in studying diversity on campus. This is followed by two chapters focusing on theoretical issues underlying diversity assessments. Yolanda Moses addresses perceptions of conflict between diversity and institutional excellence, arguing that traditional definitions of excellence are narrow and exclusionary. Antonia Darder makes a case for institutional research as a tool for cultural democracy by explicitly recognizing issues of culture and power. Three chapters on methodology follow. Henry Ingle describes a portfolio system of assessment. Penny Edgert describes the California Postsecondary Education studies cited elsewhere in this paper, and Marsha Hirano-Nakanishi describes a way of framing studies of diversity within the Total Quality Management model. A chapter by the editors on resources, both print and electronic, available to researchers completes the work.

====

Smith, D. G., L. E. Wolf, and D. E. Morrison. 1995. Paths to success: Factors related to the impact of women's colleges. *Journal of Higher Education* 66:245–266.

This study updates and expands Smith's (1990) analysis of CIRP data for women at women's colleges and private coeducational institutions. Using multiple regression and path analysis with data from the 1986 entry and 1990 follow-up of the CIRP, the authors developed a five-stage causal model predicting level of academic and extracurricular involvement from institutional gender, student perceptions of institutional priorities, and background characteristics. A final stage of the model considers the impact of the variables on a number of goal and outcome variables. The most significant result of the regression analysis was the positive impact attendance at a women's college has on student success. The path analysis indicated that while institutional gender is not a direct predictor of the outcomes of interest, the indirect effects are significant. The findings are discussed in terms of the indirect effects' role in the differential campus climate between women's colleges and private, four-year coeducational colleges.

====

Smith, E., and W. Davidson, II. 1992. Mentoring and development of African American graduate students. *Journal of College Student Development* 33:531–539.

This article attempts to determine the role that faculty and peer mentoring play in predicting the professional development of African American graduate and professional students. A survey instrument measuring peer networking, faculty mentoring, and professional development was administered to African American graduate students at a predominantly white university—182 students responded. Using multiple regression, the researchers determined the independent variables that were significant in predicting aspects of professional development. Level of mentoring was a significant predictor of teaching, research, and grantsmanship activity. Level of mentoring was not a significant predictor of conference activities or publishing. This study confirms what many believe about the importance of mentoring activities in the development of graduate students.

—

Smith, K. M. 1992. Gender differences and the impact of college on white students' racial attitudes. Ph.D. dissertation, University of Michigan, Ann Arbor.
A longitudinal study of 485 white students during their first year at a major university found that male attitudes toward policies such as affirmative action grew more negative while women's attitudes grew more positive. While the men were more influenced by perceptions about the campus climate, the women were influenced by course experiences and their own cognitive understanding of the issues.

—

Solberg, V., K. Choi, S. Ritsma, and A. Jolly. 1994. Asian American college students: It is time to reach out. *Journal of College Student Development* 35:296–302.
The authors explore the likelihood that Asian American college students seeking help on interpersonal concerns will utilize various support services. The purpose of the study was to determine if acculturation has a significant influence on where students seek support. The responses of approximately 600 Asian American students identifying with one of the five major Asian ethnic groups were selected for the survey. Students were asked to respond to a list of thirty on- and off-campus sources of help, selecting from one of three responses to each source: unlikely, maybe, and likely. Because the responses were not normally distributed, a non-parametric measure was used to assess whether there were differences in use of a help source based on cultural identification. The research found that Asian American students who have a low identification with the majority are more likely to seek help than had been thought based on earlier research. Students with low identification with the majority showed a likelihood of seeking help, both within their own community and from general university sources. The implication for practice is that help sources in colleges and universities might increase their service to members of Asian American groups by targeting services specifically to this population, taking advantage of both the disposition to seek help within the community and from general sources.

—

Solorzano, D. G. 1995a. The baccalaureate origins of Chicana and Chicano Doctorates in the Social Sciences. *Hispanic Journal of Behavioral Sciences* 17:3–32.
In studying the baccalaureate origins of Chicanas and Chicanos who earned a Ph.D. between 1980 and 1990, it was found that a few small, mostly private institutions in the Southwest were major producers of graduates who continued on to received their Ph.D.s in the social sciences.

—

——. 1995b. The doctorate production and baccalaureate origins of African Americans in the sciences and engineering. *Journal of Negro Education* 64:15–32.
This study addresses the low numbers of African American students in doctoral programs and low number of African American faculty in American higher education. The author shows that African American women and men continue to remain underrepresented in higher education, but especially so in science and engineering. The historically African American institutions still graduate the most African American

graduates in the fields of science and engineering. More research is proposed for this area.

═══

Southern Education Foundation. 1995. *Report of the panel on educational opportunity and postsecondary desegregation.* Atlanta, GA.

This multi-institutional, multi-state analysis reviews the efforts of twelve formerly segregated states to demonstrate an acceptable level of success in desegregating their higher education systems. The study describes these efforts as well as model programs used by institutions to improve access, retention, and graduation of minorities in each state. Also included are implications and recommendations for the future.

═══

Sparks, W. G., and M. E. Verner. 1993. *Intervention strategies in multicultural education: A comparison of pre-service models.* Normal: Illinois State University. ERIC, ED 354234.

In an attempt to compare the effects of two multicultural education intervention strategies (an integrated model and a subject-specific model), researchers measured the knowledge and attitudes of pre-service teacher education students in both a classroom and a field-based setting. The study took place at a regional, public university in Illinois. The goal of this research is to determine specific interventions to successfully reduce prejudicial attitudes and increase multicultural knowledge of pre-service teachers. The integration model is offered as an elective to most education majors at the institution. It includes an entry level course that deals with the broad issues of multicultural education, followed by a field experience course that places the students in different communities. The subject-specific model also entails a two course sequence; however, it is designed specifically for physical education majors. Consequently, the first course provides an overview of selected historical and cultural concepts and their relation to physical education. The second course is a discipline-based field experience that allows the pre-service physical education students to apply concepts in a field-based setting. The researchers administered a pre- and post-test assessment about students' knowledge and understanding of multicultural issues. The results indicate that students who were exposed to both methods of multicultural education through coursework increased their level of multicultural understanding. However, exposure to multicultural issues through field work was not particularly effective in helping the pre-service teachers gain a higher multicultural tolerance level.

═══

Spelman College. 1997. Faculty/student forums. In *DiversityWeb leaders' guide* [online]. Available at http://www.inform.umd.edu/DiversityWeb/Leadersguide/SED/spelman.html.

This is the protocol from a series of monthly student-faculty discussions on diversity at Spelman College that began in 1994. Readings were assigned and forums held on a host of diversity topics including: "Multiculturalism in the Liberal Arts Curriculum;" "Disability as Difference;" "Sexuality as Difference;" "Sexuality and Pedagogy;" "Religious Diversity;" and "Cross Cultural Sexualities." The project began with the help of a facilitator but continued with faculty leadership. In the second year of the project, faculty reported on the success of incorporating the issues into the classroom as well as other considerations that arose during the first year. Many students helped to compile a bibliography of resources on diversity.

Spitzburg, I. J., and V. V. Thorndike. 1992. *Creating community on college campuses.* Albany: State University of New York Press.

The authors conducted a comprehensive analysis of the current state of community on college campuses. They focused on themes of tolerance and intolerance of difference, the authority of the institution, and the connections or lack of connections between and among students and faculty. The book concludes with recommendations for creating pluralistic communities on college campuses. The goals will not be easily attained, but the implementation process will be valuable. An extensive bibliography is included.

===

Springer, L., B. Palmer, P. T. Terenzini, E. T. Pascarella, and A. Nora. 1996. Attitudes toward campus diversity: Participation in a racial or cultural awareness workshop. *Review of Higher Education* 20:53–68.

Seventeen colleges and universities in ten states participated in a study to assess the effects of awareness programs on the attitudes of white students towards diversity on campus. The study consisted of an initial data collection with two subsequent data collections. It began with 2,813 students selected at random from an eligible population of 16,561 to represent the white first-year undergraduates in the fall of 1992. In analyzing certain research questions, the study found that both sex and major were significantly related with students' attitudes towards diversity before college, with women and students in liberal arts majors having more favorable pre-college attitudes. It also found that students who stayed in more conservative majors during the first two years of college were significantly less likely to participate in racial or cultural awareness workshops. One limitation of the study was the absence of information on the workshops—whether they were voluntary or mandatory. Also, no explanation is given as to how or why attitudes change after participation in a racial or cultural awareness program. The study implies that different attitudes towards diversity based on gender and/or major are separate and not based, for example, on a high concentration of women in liberal arts majors. The authors conclude that "leaders on campus might be able to improve their racial climate by promoting participation in a racial or cultural awareness workshop."

===

Stage, F., and F. Hamrick. 1994. Diversity issues: Fostering campuswide development of multiculturalism. *Journal of College Student Development* 35:331–336.

Stage and Hamrick propose a model for developing and practicing activities on the college campus to foster an appreciation for and valuing of diversity. Building on a model of moral development, the authors illustrate how a campus can turn its words into deeds in dealing with issues of diversity.

===

Stake, J. E., and M. A. Gerner. 1987. The women's studies experience: Personal and professional gains for women and men. *Psychology of Women Quarterly* 11:277–284.

Using a pre- and post-test design, researchers studied the impact on both male and female students of enrolling in an introductory women's studies course. The study utilized a self-esteem scale as well as a survey addressing educational and job certainty and motivation. The results of a bivariate analysis indicate that both men and women in women's studies courses demonstrated greater gains in self-esteem and in job motivation and job certainty when compared to a control group. The study demonstrated the positive impact of women's studies courses for both men and women.

Stark, J., and A. Thomas, eds. 1994. *ASHE reader series: Assessment, program evaluation*. New York: Simon and Schuster.
This reader on program evaluation and assessment provides over forty classic articles on these topics from a variety of perspectives. It covers many of the basic methodological issues in evaluating impact and assessing student outcomes.

Stassen, M. L. A. 1995. White faculty members and racial diversity: A theory and its implications. *Review of Higher Education* 18:361–391.
This paper presents a theory, based on an extensive review of the literature, of white faculty members' ambivalent attitudes toward diversity. These ambivalent racial attitudes are conceptualized as stemming from socialized beliefs and cognitive processing tendencies. These tendencies are activated in a particular context, which has attitude activation effects and normative influence effects. The result of these effects on the faculty members' tendencies will result in particular behaviors in support of or in opposition to diversity. There is an extensive discussion of the role these attitudes play in the success or failure of interventions institutions may take to improve campus climate for diversity.

Steele, C. M. 1997. A threat in the air: How stereotypes shape intellectual identity and performance. *American Psychologist* 52:613–629.
This article discusses how stereotype threat impacts the achievement of African Americans and women. The author defines stereotype threat as a situational pressure, one that is "in the air," and affects confident students more than unconfident ones. A series of experiments produced several findings: 1) women significantly under-performed in relation to equally qualified men on a difficult math test, but performed just as well as equally qualified men on an advanced literature test; 2) women performed worse than men when told that a particular test produced gender differences, but performed equal to men when the test was presented as insensitive to gender differences; 3) African American participants greatly under-performed compared to white participants on a test presented as ability-diagnostic, but equaled them under nondiagnostic conditions; 4) critical feedback to African American students was strongly motivating when it was coupled with optimism about their potential; 5) having African American college students repeatedly advocate the expandability of intelligence to their elementary school tutees significantly improved their own grades; and 6) African American students showed almost no under-performance in a program described as competitive, but performed worse than other groups in a large remediation program.

Steele, C. M., and J. Aronson. 1995. Stereotype threat and the intellectual test performance of African Americans. *Journal of Personality and Social Psychology* 69:797–811.
The authors write about stereotype threat, a situation in which anything that one does that matches the stereotype of the group to which one belongs, serves to confirm that stereotype both for others and for oneself. Stereotype threat exists for any and all groups for which negative stereotypes exist. Steele and Aronson use four studies of intellectual test performance of African Americans to confirm the existence of stereotype threat. Stereotype threat is illustrated by the finding that African Americans students perform better on an IQ test when told that the test is not a measure of

intelligence but of some factor that is not so evaluative. The authors suggest that for African American students, taking a test that is supposed to measure intelligence may cause them to perform less well because of their internalization of the stereotype. All four of the studies in this article confirm the hypothesis that the existence of negative stereotypes can actually impair performance on measures of intellectual ability. The authors note that although stereotype threat is a problem associated with ethnicity and gender, they do not suggest that the problems are rooted in group membership, but rather are psychological and can be changed.

Steward, R. J. 1993. Two faces of academic success: Case studies of American Indians on a predominantly Anglo university campus. *Journal of College Student Development* 34:191–196.
The researcher sought to gain some understanding of the factors that contribute to the success of American Indian students on a predominantly white campus. Only two students on a 26,000 student campus fit the profile for study—first college experience within five years of the study, continuous enrollment since freshman year, age nineteen or less at original enrollment, and expected to graduate within one year. The participants completed a variety of surveys of demographics, preferences, competencies, alienation, support, and interpersonal behavior preferences. Results are reported both in tabular and case format. The analysis of these case studies suggests the need for university faculty and staff to develop an understanding that there is not a common model for American Indian students and their activity and involvement in the university. The researcher also suggests opportunities for further research on factors around American Indian students in higher education.

Steward, R., S. Germain, and J. Jackson. 1992. Alienation and interactional style: A style of successful Anglo, Asian, and Hispanic university students. *Journal of College Student Development* 33:149–156.
Using several instruments, the researchers explore the relationship of students' interpersonal behavioral and interaction style with the sense of alienation and success at the university. The population studied included fifty-one white students, twenty Latino/a students, and twenty-two Asian American students. Analysis of the various measures find that successful white, Asian American, and Latino/a students have similar styles of interaction and all of the groups experience alienation at the same level. The findings of this research are different from much of the literature that finds heightened levels of alienation for students of color at predominantly white colleges and universities. The authors suggest factors that may have mitigated the alienation within the groups being studied, such as acculturation to white communities.

Stewart, G. 1994. Importance and satisfaction with mentors in attainment of highest collegiate degree. Paper presented at Minority Student Today: Recruitment, Retention, and Success, November, at San Antonio, TX.
This study questions student affairs professionals about how important they felt mentoring was while attaining their highest academic degree, and how satisfied they were with their mentors. Eighty percent or more rated mentoring important or very important. The review of the literature also discusses the impact of mentoring.

Stoecker, J., E. T. Pascarella, and L. M. Wolfle. 1988. Persistence in higher education: A 9-year test of a theoretical model. *Journal of College Student Development* 29:196–209.
A national, nine-year multi-institutional study supports Tinto's model of the persistence-withdrawal process and suggests that the most important determinants of persistence are the student's academic and social integration at the institution. The overall sample, obtained from the Cooperative Institutional Research Program, comprised 5,240 individuals: 2,021 white men, 381 African American men, 2,312 white women, and 526 African American women. The sample was measured on six variables, including pre-college characteristics, pre-college commitments, institutional characteristics, college major, college academic and social integration, and persistence/withdrawal behavior.

Sue, S., and S. Okazaki. 1990. Asian American educational achievements: A phenomenon in search of an explanation. *American Psychologist* 45:913–920.
The authors examine hereditary and cultural factors that might influence the educational achievement of Asian American students. They suggest that educational achievement may be, in part, a function of perceived and experienced barriers to Asian American participation in non-education careers.

Sultana, Q. 1993. Evaluation of multicultural education in a preservice teacher education program. Paper presented at the annual meeting of the Mid-South Education Research Association, November, at New Orleans, LA.
This study attempts to ascertain the extent to which education students at Eastern Kentucky University, which follows the National Council for the Accreditation of Teacher Education (NCATE) standards as they pertain to multicultural education, understand and appreciate the concepts of multicultural education. To assess the impact of multicultural education on students, the investigators surveyed 115 teacher education students in the fall 1992 semester. Each student was given a sheet of paper with the prompt "Multicultural education is ..." and was asked to write an essay. Four researchers created a scoring guide to compare student definitions with the definition accepted by the State of Kentucky. The results indicated that 65 percent are aware of cultural differences, 19 percent know nothing of them, and 10 percent have some understanding of diversity. Researchers concluded that despite attempts to include multicultural education in a variety of courses, the level of awareness of cultural differences was not yet sufficient.

Tafalla, R. J., R. Rivera, and B. Tuchel. 1993. Psychological factors related to minority persistence on a predominantly white campus. Paper presented at Minority Student Today: Recruitment, Retention, and Success, October, at San Antonio, TX.
Ninety-five undergraduates and twenty-three permanent dropouts at a primarily white university, from an original sample of 400 students, completed thirty-one items that examined opinions about isolation on campus, discrimination, institutional support for minorities, feelings about university life, and academic satisfaction. Analysis of their replies showed three powerful influences: feelings of cultural isolation, institutional support for minorities, and academic satisfaction. Analysis comparing the sixty-one

white, twenty-seven Asian American, sixteen Latino/a, nine American Indian, and five African American respondents revealed that race affected the cultural isolation and institutional support responses. Racial subgroups did not differ significantly on the academic satisfaction measure, but the combined minorities scored lower than the white students on all three measures. Further analyses indicates that the students who had ever considered dropping out of school scored lower on the three measures than did their counterparts. However, the dropouts did not differ from the continuing students on these measures. When ten-year graduation rates were calculated for each racial group and rank ordered, the ranks were identical to the ranks for each racial group on the cultural isolation measure.

Tan, D. L. 1995. Perceived importance of role models and its relationship with minority student satisfaction and academic performance. *NACADA Journal* 15 (1): 48–51.

For this study, the author surveyed a sample of undergraduate African American and Asian American students at predominantly white universities about their perceptions of the value of role models from within the faculty, staff, and administration. The research questions included the perceived importance of role models (of the same or other race) to minority students, the presence or absence of role models, and the relationship between the perceived importance, presence, or absence of role models and satisfaction with college and academic performance. Eighty percent of the sample perceived the importance of role models, although only 58 percent reported having role models. Information on the impact of role models is inconclusive because the sample was small, although within the sample, academic performance of students with role models was actually lower than students without role models.

Tanaka, G. K. 1996. The impact of multiculturalism on white students. Ph.D. dissertation, University of California, Los Angeles. Abstract in *Dissertation Abstracts International* 57 (05): 1980A.

This dissertation used the CIRP dataset to examine the impact of multiculturalism, defined through four components—student racial diversity, institutional emphasis on a multicultural environment, the inclusion of racial-ethnic issues in the curriculum, and faculty racial diversity—on the sense of community, cultural awareness, desire to promote racial understanding, and satisfaction with college of white students. A cohort of 25,000 students at 159 institutions were included in the sample, originally surveyed in 1985 with a 1989 follow-up. Two institutional approaches have positive effects on student outcomes—institutional efforts to create a multicultural environment and to include ethnic/racial material in the curriculum. Student and faculty diversity have negative effects on white students' sense of community on campus. Participation in fraternities and sororities heighten the negative and lessen the positive effects of multiculturalism. Participation in cross-cultural activities enhances the positive and diminishes the negative effects of multiculturalism. The study suggests several approaches for institutions: develop planned and coordinated approaches to multiculturalism, involve white students in multicultural activities, and develop identities for white students that are not based on race/ethnicity.

Tate, D. S., and C. L. Schwartz. 1993. Increasing the retention of American Indian students in professional programs in higher education. *Journal of American Indian Education* 33 (1): 21–31.

A national survey of American Indians in social work programs was conducted to investigate factors impeding retention. For the eighty-four respondents, 27 percent of the total population of American Indian social work students in the U. S., the most common factors impeding retention were difficulties in acculturation, problems associated with being a non-traditional student, and the lack of faculty support.

Tatum, B. D. 1992. Talking about race, learning about racism: The application of racial identity development theory in the classroom. *Harvard Educational Review* 62 (1): 1–24.

In this article, Tatum discusses the impact of a course designed to provide students with an understanding of the psychological causes and emotional reality of racism as it appears in everyday life. Having taught the course eighteen times at three different institutions, including a large public university, a small state college, and a private women's college, the author found it had a powerful impact. In evaluations students repeatedly described the course as one of the most valuable educational experiences of their college careers.

——. 1994. Teaching white students about racism: The search for white allies and the restoration of hope. *Teachers College Record* 95:462–476.

The author examines the process of racial identity development experienced by white students in a classroom context using student voices and theory. The author also suggests ways of responding to resistance as it emerges in classroom contexts.

——. Forthcoming. *Why are all the black kids sitting together in the cafeteria and other conversations about racial identity.* New York: Basic Books.

Tatum's book approaches the topic of "self-segregation" in the context of racial identity theory and issues of racism in the society. Within this theoretical framework, she describes campus-based efforts to support students of color and simultaneous efforts to encourage intergroup conversations about race and racism. She cites research that suggests that curricular and programmatic efforts can be quite successful for all students. She cautions that the conditions for dialogue and support for students of color are not mutually exclusive.

Taylor, S. H. 1994. Enhancing tolerance: The confluence of moral development with the college experience. Ph.D. dissertation, University of Michigan. Abstract in *Dissertation Abstracts International* 56 (01): 0114A.

This dissertation looked at how college experiences contribute to moral development and tolerance for diversity among a cohort of white students at a large Midwestern university. The researcher used a survey upon entering the institution and a follow-up survey at the end of the second year of enrollment. The model proposes that tolerance for diversity is associated with a higher level of moral development which is affected by meaningful involvement in college activities and experiences, as well as pre-college experiences. The author finds that enhanced tolerance is the result of two cognitive, interpersonal moral orientations—causal and empathic thinking. For men and women there was a significant impact of college experiences on tolerance of diversity. There were also differences between the impact of various experiences on men and women and in the initial attitudes toward diversity of men and women.

=

Terrell, M., and S. Hassell. 1994. Mentoring undergraduate minority students: An overview, survey, and model program. In *Minorities in education*, edited by M. A. Wunsch. New Directions for Teaching and Learning, no. 57. San Francisco: Jossey-Bass.

The authors explain how mentors help students of color navigate the college experience and so help them deal with the frustration that students encounter in higher education institutions. The authors review the literature on the impact of mentoring programs. A group of thirty-eight institutions whose representatives participated in the "Creating Success Through Caring" program at Western Michigan University in 1989 supplied data about their mentoring programs. Almost 82 percent of the institutions had mentoring programs specifically designed for students of color and 73 percent had programs that dealt with academic performance. Almost half of the programs concentrated on the first-year experience. Most programs had a combination of faculty, staff, peers, and alumni/ae to mentor students. Retention rates ranged form 64 to 98 percent. Three institutions reported a 75 percent retention rate and two institutions achieved a 90 percent retention rate. The Northeastern Illinois University Minority Student Mentoring Program is described as a model program. At the end of the second term in this program, 92 percent of the mentees were still enrolled, while only 62 percent of the students who did not participate in mentoring remained. Only 8 percent of the mentees were on academic probation as compared to 26 percent for the non-participants still enrolled.

=

Thompson, B. W., and S. Tyagi. 1993. *Beyond a dream deferred: Multicultural education and the politics of excellence*. Minneapolis: University of Minnesota Press.

The ideological background of multiculturalism in higher education is central to many of the articles discussed in this book. The book includes important discussions of attempts to develop multicultural curricular responses. Results from the important Berkeley "Diversity Project Study" are contextualized against a background of near panic over the meaning of multiculturalism.

=

Thompson, C., and B. Fretz. 1991. Conceptualizing the adjustment and persistence of black students at predominantly white institutions. Paper presented at the annual meeting of the American Educational Research Association, April, at Chicago, IL.

This study reviews the literature which empirically tested factors contributing to African American student adjustment and retention at predominantly white American colleges and universities. The literature review covers studies involving students enrolled in four-year liberal arts institutions defined as predominantly white. It provides recommendations for future research, including the use of path models, variables not considered previously, and consideration of campus climate.

=

Tierney, W. G. 1993. *Building communities of difference. Higher education in the twenty-first century*. Westport, CT: Bergin and Garvey.

This theoretical treatise uses case studies to illustrate the author's key points about building a sense of community out of the diverse constituencies that will comprise higher education in the 21st century. Issues of educational empowerment, culture, alienation and voice, critical leadership and decision making, the public roles and private lives of gay faculty, cultural citizenship, and educational democracy are addressed within the framework of building educational institutions for the next century organized around and responsive to the needs of diverse groups of students.

——

——, ed. 1990. *Assessing academic climates and cultures.* New Directions for Institutional Research, no. 68. San Francisco: Jossey-Bass.

This volume contains seven chapters by various authors on aspects of campus climate and culture that will be of interest to institutional researchers. Topics include the relationship of an understanding of campus climate and culture to organizational effectiveness; the need for new presidents to understand institutional cultures, student cultures, and faculty cultures; methodological issues relating to assessing campus cultures and climates through surveys and ethnographic auditing; and an annotated resource guide to the analysis, interpretation, and utilization of culture and climate.

——

Townsend, L. 1994. How universities successfully retain and graduate African American students. *Journal of Blacks in Higher Education* 1 (4): 85–89.

This article describes retention efforts for African American students at several historically black colleges and universities and predominantly white institutions which have higher than average African American persistence rates. The central role of the faculty, both in and out of the classroom, is emphasized, as is the importance of adequate student financial aid.

——

Treisman, P. U. 1988. A study of the mathematics performance of black students at the University of California, Berkeley. In *Changing the culture: Mathematics education in the research community*, edited by N. D. Fisher, H. B. Keynes, and P. D. Wagreich. CBMS Issues in Mathematics Education, vol. 5. American Mathematical Society.

Treisman tells the story of the creation of the Mathematics Workshop at the University of California, Berkeley. As a mathematics faculty member, he was interested in learning why African American students were not successful in introductory mathematics courses. These courses serve as a gateway to all science and engineering majors, the declared major of many African American students at the university. Treisman interviewed and observed African American students and Chinese students attempting to discover what factors might account for significant differences in their success in introductory mathematics programs. He found that due to a variety of cultural reasons, African American students felt the need to work things out for themselves while Chinese students typically joined peer study groups in mathematics. While the study groups were organized around mathematics, they served a larger function for participants. The groups not only provided information about mathematics, but gave support to students in other areas of university life. The pilot mathematics project at Berkeley organized a small group of African American students into a study group with which Treisman worked. The group offered students help in mathematics, but it also provided them with a better understanding of what was required to succeed, not only in mathematics, but in the university at large. The students in the pilot project were successful and Treisman took what he discovered from this project to develop the Mathematics Project.

===

Trigg, M. K., and B. J. Balliet. 1997. Finding community across boundaries: Service learning in women's studies. In *Democratic education in an age of difference: Redefining citizenship in higher education*, edited by R. Guarasci and G. H. Cornwell. San Francisco: Jossey-Bass.

The authors describe a program that links women's studies with community service as a way of broadening the students' understanding of how diversity impacts on feminism. Within a feminist perspective, students are encouraged to explore the diversity of women's experiences and ways of understanding. Student reflections on their experiences are used to assess the success of the program. Students report a growing understanding of diverse women's experiences.

===

Trippi, J., and H. E. Cheatham. 1989. Effects of special counseling programs for black freshmen on a predominantly white campus. *Journal of College Student Development* 30:35–40.

This study examines which student characteristics and features of specialized counseling are related to African American students' academic performance, persistence in college, and persistence in college degree status. Specific student characteristics and descriptive characteristics of a special counseling program are found to be positively related to African American students' persistence in college and degree status, including the incidence of in-person contacts, the importance of initial contact, active resolution of short-range concerns using action-oriented interactions, and recognition of the limited utility of intrusive counseling.

===

Troutt, B. 1992. Silence: A factor in the nontraditional student's academic performance. *Journal of College Student Development* 33: 87–90.

The author reviews literature identifying a number of factors in nontraditional student cultural backgrounds which may encourage their silence in the classroom. These factors include: the non-assertive behavior taught by American Indian parents to their children; respect for authority of Latino/a cultures; or the anxiety of African American students. The author suggests several interventions to be practiced at the classroom or even institutional level to give voice to otherwise silent students.

===

Turner, C. S. V. 1994. Guests in someone else's house: Students of color. *Review of Higher Education* 17:355–370.

This paper describes how students of color at the University of Minnesota perceive the campus climate. Participants in the study were primarily first generation college students who had participated in minority support programs. Study results show that the campus climate is "unwelcoming" to students of color. Participants describe their quality of life as intimidating, lonely, and exclusionary. Study participants state that supportive organizations play an important role in helping to alleviate their isolation. However, after leaving this safe environment, the climate once again becomes unwelcoming. Another finding is that staff of color experience burn-out, stress, and bitterness because their function is to help support at-risk undergraduate students while they themselves are at risk. The respondents also provide suggestions to help make their campus more welcoming.

═══

Twombly, S. B. 1995. Gendered images of community college leadership: What messages they send. In *Gender and power in the community college*, edited by B. K. Townsend. New Directions for Community Colleges, no. 89. San Francisco: Jossey-Bass.

This article reviews the evolution of leadership in community colleges. The author asks, "Can we afford to continue with a male-dominated theory of leadership at the community college?" Twombly suggests a womanist perspective and provides various strategies to combat sexism at community colleges.

═══

Ugbolue, A., P. N. Whitley, and P. J. Stevens. 1987. Examination of a pre-entrance enrichment program for minority students admitted to medical school. *Journal of Medical Education* 62:8–16.

This is a study of 206 minority students who attended Boston University School of Medicine as first-year students from 1973 through 1984. One hundred fifteen had participated in a six week pre-entrance enrichment program (PEP) and 91 had not. Analyses indicate that although the participants had lower Medical College Admissions Test scores upon entrance to medical school than did the minority nonparticipants, they received a higher proportion of better grades in two first-year subjects and did somewhat better than the minority nonparticipants in six of the remaining seven first-year subjects. Of the twenty-seven participants who replied to pre- and postprogram questionnaires, most indicated that they had gained benefits from the PEP. The ten participants who completed an end of the first year questionnaire reported fewer academic adjustment problems than did the ten minority nonparticipants who completed the questionnaire.

═══

University of California. n.d. *Special report on University of California development programs for undergraduate students.* Berkeley, CA.

This report explores a number of program areas and the university's history with these programs. It describes program backgrounds, strategy and performance outcomes of selected system-wide programs for pre-college students, and performance outcomes of selected campus-based programs for undergraduates. It also presents the latest trend information of underrepresented students at the University of California. Both enrollment and retention indicators show system-wide improvement.

═══

University of Wisconsin, Stevens Point. 1992. *Which one of your ten friends is homosexual?: Understanding, accepting, and supporting.* National Association of College and University Residence Halls Report, no. N25D–92–005–12. Stevens Point: University of Wisconsin, Stevens Point [online]. Available at http://www.nacurh.okstate.edu/rfi/rfi_frame.html.

This is a report on an awareness program conducted at University of Wisconsin, Stevens Point. The program was a panel discussion with questions from the audience. The diversity of the panel helped to convey the issues. The panel included parents of gay and lesbian children and an openly gay pastor. Extensive publicity in student newspapers helped the program's success.

Vanderpool, N., and W. Brown. 1994. Implications of a peer telephone network on adult learner GPA and retention. *Journal of College Student Development* 35:125–128.

This article looks at another group representing diversity on the college campus—adult learners on a traditional residential campus. Several factors including age and residence serve to separate this group from the more traditional college student. They may miss out on the social and informal interactions on campus, communication about campus events and services, and out-of-class intellectual and social opportunities. A large West Coast public university explored the impact of contact on the retention and GPA of adult learners. A group of peer leaders, adult students who had successfully completed at least one year at the university, made three telephone calls to new adult learner students during the Fall term. The group of students who were called were compared to a control group of students who were not called to see if there was a difference in first to second term retention and GPA. The students who were called were retained at a significantly higher level than those who were not called. There was no statistically significant difference in GPA between those who were called and those who were not called. The results are not surprising, as they support the belief that contact between the institution and the student will support retention. The model, though, might be just as applicable for any group of students as for the adult learners studied in this research.

=

Varlotta, L. 1997. Invoking a university's mission statement to promote diversity, civility, and free speech. *NASPA Journal* 34:123–133.

This article deals with the responsibility of student affairs administrators and the tools available to promote diversity on campus. In particular, the author advocates the use of the institution's mission statement to articulate the commitment of the university and to redirect existing policies and practices from "tolerance for diversity to interactive pluralism." The article begins by exploring the existing debate on diversity and outlining Astin's reasons for supporting diversity initiatives—student gains in cognitive and affective development, increased level of satisfaction with the college experience, and increased commitment to multiculturalism. The author focuses on the use of the mission statement to direct the diversity objectives of student affairs professionals. These are objectives that promote diversity programs, which in turn foster inquiry and free exchange of ideas. Lastly, the author shifts his focus to the parameters that define the free exchange of ideas, including the legal limits of free speech. He concludes by emphasizing the need to look beyond the First Amendment in promoting diversity, civility, and free speech.

=

Villalpando, O. 1994. Comparing the effects of multiculturalism and diversity on minority and white students' satisfaction with college. Paper presented at the annual meeting of the Association for the Study of Higher Education, November, at Tucson, AZ. ERIC, ED 375721.

The study looked at the differential impact of diversity initiatives on minority and white students. Using the CIRP data base which provides longitudinal data for first-year and fourth-year students, the study investigated the impact on students who attended racial/cultural awareness workshops and who socialized with someone from other racial/ethnic groups. Students who reported high levels of satisfaction were those who had participated in workshops and had faculty who included racial/ethnic materials in their courses. In addition, the college's commitment to a strong multicultural environment had a strong impact on student satisfaction regardless of the student's background.

===

———. 1996. The long-term effects of college on Chicana and Chicano students' "other oriented" values. Ph.D. dissertation, University of California, Los Angeles.

This dissertation examines the "other-oriented" humanitarian values and behavior of a group of 186 Chicano/a college students, matched with a sample of 186 white students who all responded to the 1984 CIRP survey and 1989 and 1994 follow-up studies. The dependent variables were the students' involvement in community service or volunteer activities, engagement in a service career, and commitment to other-oriented goals as measured in the ninth year after college follow-up. All of the dependent variables were pre-tested in the freshman student survey. All of the dependent variables were influenced by forms of college involvement. Chicanos are affected more than Chicanas by interacting with other Chicano/as during and after college. Chicanas are affected more by college experiences that engage them in racial/ethnic or political/social issues and participation in volunteer activities. The most important influence on future activity and attitudes for white students is participation in volunteer activities. White males, like Chicanos, are influenced by interacting with other same race students, but the effect on after college values is negative.

===

Vogel, S. A., and P. B. Adelman. 1992. The success of college students with learning disabilities: Factors related to educational attainment. *Journal of Learning Disabilities* 25:430–441.

Vogel and Adelman compare the educational attainment of sixty-two students with learning disabilities to a sample of fifty-eight peers matched on gender and ACT composite scores. They found the college exit GPA and graduation rate of the learning disabilities group was slightly, though not significantly, higher than the control group, even though the control group had higher entering reading and written language skills. This finding was attributed to a strong advising system for students with learning disabilities. The study also found that the learning disabled group took a lighter academic load and an additional year—six rather than five years—to complete their degree.

===

Walters, A. S. 1994. Using visual media to reduce homophobia: A classroom demonstration. *Journal of Sex Education and Therapy* 20 (2): 92–100.

The study describes an intervention designed to reduce homophobia within a group of college students. A pre- and post-test measure of homophobia and empathy to homosexuals was administered to two groups of college students enrolled in sections of a human sexuality course. Both groups received the same lectures and participated in similar course discussions. One group also received a presentation and a slide show, providing a historical account of the treatment of gay characters in film. A lecture accompanying the slide presentation discussed the different treatment of homosexuals and homosexual themes when compared to heterosexuals and heterosexual themes. The group receiving the slide show showed a significant decrease in homophobia and a significant increase in empathy for homosexuals after seeing the slide show. Comments from students in the treated group call for the slide show to be repeated in future sections and note that the students are not threatened by the information in the presentation.

=

Walters, A. S., and C. P. Phillips. 1994. Hurdles: An activity for homosexuality educa-
    tion. *Journal of Sex Education and Therapy* 20 (3): 198–203.
This paper reports on various and conflicting processes of coming out as lesbian, gay, or bisexual. The work makes the point that coming out is not a one-time event but happens in new and diverse social circumstances. The paper reports on an activity designed to help people working with students to be aware of the difficulties and challenges of coming out, especially for lesbian and gay youth. This activity attempts to build self-esteem.

=

Wang, Y., W. Sedlacek, and F. Westbrook. 1992. Asian Americans and student orga-
    nizations: Attitudes and participation. *Journal of College Student Development*
    33:214–221.
The authors explore the attitudes of Asian American students toward involvement in student organizations, especially those with a pre-professional, academic focus. They attempt to determine if there are differences in these attitudes among the various groups of Asian American students. Approximately 50 percent of the Asian American students at a large university were surveyed. Eighty percent of those surveyed responded to the questionnaire. The survey elicited student responses to twenty-nine questions about involvement in various kinds of campus organizations and activities. In general, students reported mixing with white students and not feeling isolated or left out. Although they agreed with participation in minority groups, they did not agree with pre-professional groups made of Asians alone or with ethnic sub-groups. There were significant differences in responses from students identifying with different Asian American ethnic sub-groups. This study supports the argument that the Asian American ethnic group is not monolithic, but is composed of multiple subgroups with different attitudes and needs.

=

Washington Center. 1995. *Cultural pluralism project final report*. Seattle: University of
    Washington.
This report describes the three-year cultural pluralism project of the Washington Center to incorporate the study of United States pluralism into general education and core curricula of twenty-six colleges and universities. The curriculum project emerged out of state-wide concerns for underrepresentation and campus climate. These curricular efforts were seen as part of other institutional diversity initiatives and were to be part of a larger planning process. A number of campuses in the project had articulated student outcomes which were to result from the curricular changes and most of the developed courses had clear student outcomes imbedded in the structure of the course. No information was available about the results of those analyses; studies were in the formative stage. The report documents, however, the impact of these efforts on institutional change.

=

Watanabe, G. C. 1992. A comprehensive developmentally-based undergraduate diver-
    sity education model at Washington State University. Ed.D. dissertation,

Washington State University. Abstract in *Dissertation Abstracts International* 53 (11): 3825A.

This dissertation assesses the impact of programming in a residence hall designed to deal with a broad range of diversity issues including racism, sexism, homophobia, ageism, ableism, and socioeconomic status. Pre- and post-tests of student attitudes and opinions were made using quantitative instruments and a structured interview to assess change in students on measures of intercultural sensitivity, moral development, and social interaction. The treatment between the pre- and post-test was diversity education programming conducted by student trainers. There was significant positive change in some areas, although the size of the sample limits the significance of the results.

Watson, L., and G. Kuh. 1996. The influences of dominant race environments on student involvement, perceptions, and educational gains: A look at historically black and predominantly white liberal arts institutions. *Journal of College Student Development* 37:415–420.

The relationship between involvement in campus activities, perceptions of the institutional environment, and educational gains of undergraduates at two predominantly black and two predominately white liberal arts institutions were examined. African American students at the predominantly black institutions benefited more from their overall involvement compared with white students and African American students at predominantly while institutions.

Wells, J. W. 1991. What makes a difference?: Various teaching strategies to reduce homophobia in university students. *Annals of Sex Research* 4 (3/4): 229–238.

Students participating in a human sexuality course were administered three different instruments, the Index of Homophobia, the Homosexual Behaviors Inventory, and the Self-Esteem Scale, five times over the course of a semester. A variety of methods of teaching about homosexuality including lecture, film, and panel discussion were employed in the course. Throughout the semester, mean scores indicate that homophobia decreased and self-esteem increased for students who participated in the course. It was not possible to identify a specific approach to teaching about homosexuality that had a more or less significant impact on students. It is interesting to note that the impact of the first twenty-four course sessions in which the instructors modeled an acceptance of the varieties of sexual activity was as great as the change that occurred following the four course sessions that dealt specifically with homosexuality.

Wells-Lawson, M. 1994. The effects of race and type of institution on the college experiences of black and white undergraduate students attending thirty predominantly black and predominantly white colleges and universities. Paper presented at the annual meeting of the American Educational Research Association, April, at New Orleans, LA.

This study looks at differences between white students at predominantly black colleges and African American students at predominantly white colleges to determine whether, after controlling for student background characteristics, there were differences in reported grades, relations with faculty, perceptions of diversity in campus environment, and a sense of being discriminated against. Controlling for background characteristics, there were no differences in academic performance of African American and white students on African American campuses, while African American students' academic performance was significantly lower than white students' on white campuses.

===

Wenzlaff, T. L., and A. Biewer. 1996. Research: Native American students define factors for success. *Tribal College* 7 (4): 40–44.

This study reports factors contributing to the retention of ten American Indian students in a U. S. Department of Education sponsored teacher education program at North Dakota State University. The program provided monetary assistance, peer group meetings, and mentoring. Each student had an associate's degree from a North Dakota tribal college. Of the eleven students enrolled in the 1994–1995 academic year, ten returned for Fall 1995 classes. These students identified family support and mentoring, by both professors and peers, as the primary factors in their success. They also cited determination and a focus on their education as personal factors.

===

White, C. J., and C. Shelley. 1996. Telling stories: Students and administrators talk about retention. In *Leveling the playing field: Promoting academic success for African American students*, edited by I. H. Johnson and A. J. Ottens. New Directions for Sudent Services, no. 74. San Francisco: Jossey-Bass.

This article includes narratives from three students of color and a white woman. The review of the literature talks about the deculturation and objectification of students of color and women. One student states that he would feel more comfortable if his achievements were recognized. Another student states that retention is dependent on positive relationships built between students, administrators, and faculty. A student of color states that the equal opportunity bridge program and other special programs have made a difference in his life. All students were admitted to different colleges and with different admission programs. These students all encountered the same difficulties and prospered in supportive environments.

===

Whitt, E. 1994. I can be anything: Student leadership in three women's colleges. *Journal of College Student Development* 35:198–207.

To explore the factors that influenced women students as leaders in women's institutions, the author conducted research at three women's colleges. Methods of data collection included interviews with individuals and groups, observations (of meetings, ceremonies, and classes), and analyses of college documents (both internal and external, formal and informal). The goal was to gain understanding and to explain how women's colleges meet their goal of women's education, especially their role in developing women as leaders. The researcher found that women's colleges, because they have as their goal the education of women, go about their educational processes in ways that specifically encourage and support women as learners and as leaders. The article includes specific examples from each of the three colleges. Whitt suggests that there are lessons for all colleges in the approaches to education taken by women's colleges.

===

Willemsen, E. W., and J. Gainen. 1995. Revisioning statistics: A cognitive apprenticeship approach. In *Fostering student success in quantitative gateway courses*, edited by

J. Gainen and E. W. Willemsen. New Directions for Teaching and Learning, no. 61. San Francisco: Jossey-Bass.

The author of this article defines seven characteristics of courses: experiential learning, collaboration, discovery, use of authentic problems, planning before doing, risk taking, and integrative learning. These characteristics are part of a paradigm that will transform student learning of statistics. Cognitive apprenticeship is the underlying principle of this learning. This model takes real life situations from people of diverse backgrounds and incorporates these experiences into elementary statistics. This paradigm shift is necessary, the author argues, to increase achievement for all students.

===

Williams, R. 1995. Biblio-mentors: Autobiography as a tool for counseling African American males. *Journal of African American Men* 1 (3): 73–84.

Books were used to enhance discussion of the social-emotional concerns of African American males. The literature utilized in the study allowed the participants to voice concerns that may not have been previously discussed. The results show that participants developed a sense of mattering and cohesion. They were also willing to discuss personal and emotional experiences with very little encouragement. The article also cites other developmental bibliotherapy studies that reflect positive outcomes in academic achievement, self-concept, and attitude changes. Although its participants were secondary students, the study holds value to those interested in retention issues.

===

Willie, C., M. Grady, and R. Hope. 1991. *African-Americans and doctoral experience: Implications for policy.* New York: Teachers College Press.

This study examines 146 African American scholars who pursued graduate education from 1977 to 1985. All participants were faculty members at United Negro College Fund institutions and were awarded grants by the Lilly Foundation to pursue full-time study. The study shows that providing financial (fellowship) support is an effective way of increasing the supply of African American professors. This study also discusses factors that affect the rate of degree completion for African American graduate students, making it of great interest to policy makers and administrators in higher education.

===

Wilson, K. B. 1994. Developing a freshman mentoring program: A small college experience. In *Minorities in education*, edited by M. A. Wunsch. New Directions for Teaching and Learning, no. 57. San Francisco: Jossey-Bass.

The author describes the freshman mentoring program at Brewton-Park College, a community college in rural Georgia. The program includes 64 percent of the entering class, with differing ages and ethnicities. Almost 60 percent of the first year students were in need of academic assistance. Twenty seven percent of the mentees were African American males; 61 percent of the mentors were administrators and faculty members; and 39 percent of the mentors were from the local area. Sixty-four percent of the mentors were white; 35 percent of the mentors were African American. At the end of one quarter, the author found that the mentoring program helped retain 88 percent of the mentees as compared with an overall retention rate of 53 percent for students who lacked mentors.

Wolf, L. E. 1995. Models of excellence: The baccalaureate origins of successful European American women, African American women, and Latinas. Ph.D. dissertation, Claremont Graduate School, CA.

In this study, the baccalaureate origins of successful women, defined as earning a Ph.D. or being listed in *Who's Who,* were analyzed. The analysis controlled for institutional size and identified institutions which graduated disproportionate numbers of successful white, African American, and Latina women. Six institutions were selected from among the most successful for additional qualitative study. The findings demonstrated that special-focus institutions (women's colleges, historically African American colleges, and Latino/a-serving institutions) graduate a disproportionate number of successful women as compared to predominantly white coeducational institutions. The findings supported previous research on women's colleges and historically African American colleges, and provided one of the first analyses of the role of Latino/a-serving institutions. The qualitative analysis of the six sample institutions indicate that high academic expectations and support were common factors across the institutions. Other contributors to student success included the presence of role models, the importance of community service, and the power of a focused institutional mission.

Wright, B. 1990. American Indian studies programs: Surviving the '80s, thriving in the '90s. *Journal of American Indian Education* 30 (1): 17–24.

Wright examines the state of American Indian Studies programs across the country. First, he finds that as colleges develop cultural diversity requirements, these programs will fill that need. Next, faculty of these programs provide service to their institutions and provide links to American Indian communities. Finally, the programs provide support services to American Indian students on campus to improve retention.

Wright, B., and P. W. Head. 1990. Tribally controlled community colleges: A student outcomes assessment of associate degree recipients. *Community College Review* 18 (3): 28–33.

This study of the outcomes of tribal community college education surveyed over 400 graduates of Montana's seven tribally-controlled community colleges over a twelve-year period. Fifty-three percent of those surveyed responded. Nearly two-thirds of respondents indicated that they were employed at the time of the survey; an additional 10 percent were full-time students. In contrast to the general unemployment rate for the state's American Indian population, this represented significantly high levels of employment. Respondents also indicated a high level of satisfaction with their community college experience and the level of achievement of educational goals. Although the study suggest many areas for additional research, it also points to the success of tribally-controlled community colleges at meeting the educational needs of American Indian students.

Young, B., and C. Sowa. 1992. Predictors of academic success for black student athletes. *Journal of College Student Development* 33:318–324.

The authors explore the combination of cognitive and non-cognitive variables that best predict the college academic success of African American athletes. The sample numbered 136 African American students who were admitted to a predominantly white university between 1984 and 1988. Non-cognitive variables were collected from a student information sheet and cognitive variables from the student's academic record. Two dependent variables were used to measure academic success—semester and year GPA and semester and year credits completed. As expected, high school class rank and grades significantly correlate with college GPA. Of special interest is the frequent and significant correlation between long-term goals and self concept with college GPA and credits completed. Other factors, including racism, leadership, and involvement in community service, are significantly correlated with the measures of success in some terms. This study suggests that additional factors should be considered along with cognitive ones in making determinations about the likelihood of success in college of African American student athletes, and possibly all African American students in college.

=====

Zúñiga, X., and B. Nagda. 1993. Dialogue groups. In *Multicultural teaching in the university*, edited by D. Schoem, L. Frankel, X. Zúñiga, and E. Lewis. Westport, CT: Praeger.

This chapter describes the results of qualitative evaluations of student participants in a dialogue process at the University of Michigan and the structures which promote effective intergroup dialogue. The authors also emphasize that the climate of many institutions hamper efforts to bring students together. The findings suggest that dialogue groups, when effectively designed, facilitate: the opportunity to break down barriers; challenge ignorance inside and outside oneself; bring new insights and foster identity development; provoke new questions; and create the possibility for building coalitions.

=====

Zúñiga, X., B. A. Nagda, T. D. Sevig, M. Thompson, and E. L. Dey. 1995. Speaking the unspeakable: Student learning outcomes in intergroup dialogues on a college campus. Paper presented at the annual meeting of the Association for the Study of Higher Education, November, at Orlando, FL.

This empirical study compared students at the University of Michigan who participated in an intergroup dialogue program with students in related courses including women's studies and sociology. Using pre- and post-assessments of attitudes and values, the study concluded that while the intergroup dialogues were effective, there were differences based on group membership and entering attitudes in the three settings. The study also highlights the kinds of outcomes that can be investigated.

=====

Zúñiga, X., C. M. Vasques, T. D. Sevig, and B. A. Nagda. n.d. *Dismantling walls and building bridges: Student experiences in inter-race/inter-ethnic dialogues*. Available from the Program on Intergroup Relations, Conflict and Community, 3000 Michigan Union, 530 South State Street, Ann Arbor, MI 48105–1349.

This study reports on a program on inter-race/inter-ethnic dialogues conducted by the Program on Intergroup Relations Conflict and Community at the University of Michigan. The dialogues are a series of ongoing small-group discussions between members of two different groups facilitated by trained peer educators. Earlier quantitative research on students participating in dialogues has assessed the impact on learning outcomes. This study analyzes the self-reflection papers of forty participants in seven different inter-race/inter-ethnic dialogues using qualitative methods. Analysis exposed themes brought out in the quantitative pre- and post-tests thus allowing the researchers to determine whether participants experienced the themes of the groups in ways that were planned by the developers of the groups. This analysis of student reflections supports earlier findings that such dialogues contribute to the educational process.